Revolutionary Pressures in Africa

Claude Ake

Revolutionary Pressures in Africa

Claude Ake

Zed Press Ltd., 57 Caledonian Road, London N1 9DN.

Revolutionary Pressures in Africa was first published by
Zed Press, 57 Caledonian Road, London, N1 9DN in May
1978.

Copyright © Claude Ake, 1978

ISBN Hb 0 905762 14 2

ISBN Pb 0 905762 15 0

Printed by Billing & Sons Ltd., London

Typeset by Lyn Caldwell

Designed by An Dekker

CONTENTS

The saying that scholarship is a collective endeavour is surely true of this book. In the course of writing it, I have incurred a debt of gratitude to many people, too numerous to mention. Special thanks are due to my students who put up with my obsession with 'the dynamics of social forces' and contributed immensely to the development and clarification of my ideas. I am also deeply grateful to Roger van Zwanenberg, Robert Molteno and Colin Prescod whose thoughtful review of the manuscript saved me from many errors. Needless to say, I alone am responsible for those that still remain.

Claude Ake

School of Social Sciences
University Of Port Harcourt
Nigeria

July, 1977.

INTRODUCTION

In the following pages I examine the dynamics of social forces in Africa with particular attention to the question of whether the social forces are generating revolutionary pressures or whether, instead, they are aiding the consolidation of the status quo. My thesis is that, on balance, the objective conditions are such that their dynamics are moving Africa towards socialist revolution.

The argument develops as follows: In Chapter 1, I argue that (a) there is a global production system from whose contradictions arises a global class struggle between 'proletarian' and 'bourgeois' countries; and (b) this global class struggle generates strong revolutionary pressures in Africa, intensifying the mutual alienation of the African bourgeoisie and proletariat. In Chapter 2 I focus attention on one of the most salient features of Africa, namely neo-colonial dependence, because it illustrates the interaction of international and domestic social forces. This is illustrated in the context of developing the argument that neo-colonial dependence is rooted in the class structure of Africa; that it cannot be ended unless a socialist revolution occurs; that by maintaining neo-colonial dependence in accordance with the necessities of its objective situation, the African bourgeoisie promotes its own revolutionary liquidation.

In Chapter 3, I outline the class structure of contemporary Africa and attempt to show how the dynamics of class relations reduce the prospects of overcoming underdevelopment. In Chapter 4, further analysis of the dynamics of social forces in Africa, particularly class relations, is used to throw more light on the possibility of socialist revolution. I argue here that objective conditions compel the African bourgeoisie to adopt and propagate an ideology which, paradoxically, helps to develop *radical* consciousness amongst the African masses. Chapter 5, the final chapter, considers the relative prospects of capitalism and socialism. I try to show why socialist revolutions are probable in African countries, how they will occur, who will make them and what their character will be. The chapter indicates that, for Africa, the choice is not really between socialism and capitalism, but between socialism and barbarism in the most literal sense of the word.

The theoretical character of this work compels me to treat African countries in a highly undifferentiated manner. I am less interested in the historical uniqueness of particular African countries than in finding a fairly small number of related assumptions and principles which will explain as much of the African experience as possible. When my explanations and theories are confronted with historical experience, it will be found that they fit some countries and some types of experience better than others. That is as it should be. The value of what I offer here must lie not in the fact that it explains everything about every country in Africa, but that it explains much of what is happening in Africa as a whole.

Finally, I should mention that, in developing my argument, I have not bothered to make any allowance for, or concession to, the susceptibilities of any group. I am not writing to please or to comfort, but to further understanding and to stimulate thinking — hopefully constructive thinking — on our urgent predicament in Africa today.

1

THE GLOBAL CONTEXT

The major source of revolutionary pressures in Africa today is the primary contradiction of the world economic system. In this chapter I want to examine this contradiction and show how it generates strong revolutionary pressures in Africa. My point of departure is two highly problematic postulates: (a) that as an economy, the world constitutes a capitalist system and (b) that the actors in this global capitalist system are countries — some of which are analogous to individual entrepreneurs, (I call these the bourgeois countries), and others of which are analogous to the workers, (these I call proletarian countries), in a national capitalist economy. Here lies the primary global contradiction.

THE GLOBAL STRUGGLE: PROLETARIAN VERSUS BOURGEOIS COUNTRIES

Since this second postulate is the more problematic I shall begin by discussing it. To proceed according to it is to accept the validity of calling or designating countries bourgeois or proletarian, of representing countries as constituting classes which engage in a class struggle. This postulate raises questions of methodology and of the analytic value of using concepts such as bourgeois outside their original context. Also, it raises an important political question; some of the implications of this postulate are potentially reactionary. It could easily lead us to conceal the class struggle behind a titanic battle of metaphysical entities and to forget that in the final analysis it is persons who exploit or suffer exploitation.

Are class categories applicable to countries? Can we intelligibly and usefully talk of proletarian and bourgeois countries, of a class struggle between countries? Many would say no. According to the orthodox usage of the concept of class, the membership of class consists of individuals, and class relations are, in the final analysis, relations between individuals which are given their specifity by a particular mode of production. Indeed when we take account of the fact that we talk of class always in the context of a particular mode of production, we see that the applicability of class categories is even more restrictive. Thus the class categories of the capitalist mode of production apply to persons in an atomized society characterized by pervasive commodification. In the light of such considerations it would seem that the application of the concept of class to countries does violence to the concept. Countries are legal associations in a particular geographical locale. They cannot be treated as persons except by analogy, and it will be a difficult analogy at best.

However, to approach the question in this way is to build rather arbitrarily on a secondary question, namely the question of the membership of class. Since the central issue is the use of the concept of class, our point of departure should be the meaning of the concept. While the membership of class is a relevant consideration in the definition of class, it is not itself the definition. Classes are social groups, which are constituted on the basis of relations to the means of production, particularly the relationship of ownership or non-ownership of the means of production. Once we recognize this, the application of the concept of class to countries does not seem so far-fetched, since countries are also social groups. Of course this does not solve the problem of applying the concept of class to countries, but it helps to define it properly. Since it is now clear that in talking of classes we are talking not so much of persons as of social groups, especially of the relation of social groups to the means of production in a historical division of labour, our original question of usage reduces to whether the relations between countries are analogous to the relationship between the smaller social groups such as capital and labour in a national economy. In this chapter, I will make this case by spelling out the sense in which the relationship between countries is analogous to the relationship between classes and by showing how this manner of looking at things helps us to understand what is happening and what is likely to happen in Africa.

It may be objected that, even if this could be done, another serious difficulty remains, namely that this analytic approach would necessarily lead us to gloss over the class divisions within countries. For to call a social group a class is to posit the homogeneity of that social group in regard to the relation of its members to the means of production. Thus when we designate a social group as proletarian we imply that the members of this group uniformly lack the means of production, in this case capital. By the same token, to call a country a proletarian country would imply that the members of that country uniformly lack the means of production.

This mode of analysis could indeed lead one to gloss over class differences within countries. But this need not be so. It should become increasingly clear that the whole point of applying class categories and class analysis to international relations is precisely to bring into clear relief the class structure and class struggle of African societies. The application of class analysis to international relations is not a substitute for the class analysis of particular countries but a complement to it.

It is important to be clear why this complement is necessary. The need arises because of a serious defect in our methodological and theoretical tools for handling the international system. Bourgeois social science is particularly defective in this regard. Because of an understandable reluctance to draw attention to some aspects of the development of capitalism, bourgeois social science has tried to study international relations without paying much attention to imperialism. Such a manner of studying the global system can hardly be useful since the competition of imperialisms and the imperialist penetration of the world provide much of the dynamics of contemporary international relations. The approach of radical scholars, especially Marxists, is far more illuminating though still less than satisfactory. Taking Marxism-Leninism as their point of departure, they study the global system in terms of the competition of imperialisms, the penetration of the periphery and its consequences, the development of one world-wide single division of labour and two corresponding class formations. This approach is not entirely adequate because it does not register the significance of a world divided into countries which are in competition. The division of the world into countries is an important contradiction which must be carefully considered if we are to understand what is happening in particular countries and in the international system. It has important consequences for the prospects of socialist revolution in particular countries, for the ability of progressive countries to further the conquest of the world by socialism, and for the realization of socialism in particular countries. If we do not pay serious attention to this contradiction, some social phenomena will remain incomprehensible. For instance the Sino-Soviet dispute cannot be explained in terms of competing imperialisms, the global penetration of capitalism and the peripheralization of the world. Instead, many of the perplexing turns in the foreign policies of China and the Soviet Union, for instance, are related to the necessities of the Hobbesian competition among countries. The same is true of domestic policy: China cannot simply get on with the task of building socialism without paying attention to the necessities of international competition. For while it strives to build socialism, it also struggles for its survival, and for scarce goods; these struggles influence what it does, and what it can do, at home.

I say all this without prejudice to the fact that the world has to be analyzed dialectically. Countries or nation-states are not fossilized determinations. Like everything else, they too are in process. Indeed the very Hobbesian character of the competition between countries has inevitably led to monopolization, to a considerable negation of countries and the contradictions between them. More importantly the development of capitalism has contributed to the same effect. The impulse of capitalism to extend its market and the growth of monopoly capitalism may well be rendering a world of countries obsolete. Nonetheless, the fact remains that we still live in a world of countries, a world in which this division remains important. The conceptual tools with which we seek to understand the world must help us to come to terms with this present reality as well as with the new forces which are transforming it.

I will now turn to the exposition of my first postulate, regarding the capitalist character of the global system. The global system possesses all the structural features, interactional patterns, and normative characteristics of the capitalist market-place. First, the members or actors of the global market, namely countries, are primarily self-interested, each one seeking to maximize its utilities. Second, they act out their egotism by private appropriation of scarce resources. All countries defend the right of private property by their assertion of sovereignity over their territory and the natural resources within it. In fact according to the conventions of the international system, the members of a country are for all practical purposes regarded as the private property of that collectivity. Third, the principle of laisser-faire is a legitimizing norm and to some extent an operative norm of the global economy. In the contemporary international system, this principle is mainly expressed in the right of self-determination of nation-states. Of course in practice the freedoms and concrete rights associated with laisser-faire hardly exist, and this obscures the similarity between the global economy and the market-place. These freedoms dwindled precisely because laisser-faire existed in such a pure form in the international system. Obviously a faithful application of laisser-faire quickly leads to monopolization or to a dialetic negation of that principle, at any rate to a situation in which only the very strong are free to do what they can, leaving the rest to endure what they must. Fourth, the global economy is dominated by values which complement the above three features of the market-place. These values include the legitimacy of self-interested behaviour, individualism, efficiency, pragmatism, rationality, formal equality and formal freedom. The point does not call for further elaboration; as soon as the global economy is looked at as a political system, these values emerge in clear relief.

I have so far employed the general usage of the concept of capitalism. This usage corresponds to the picture of capitalist society that emerges from Adam Smith's *The Wealth of Nations* and Hegel's discussion of civil society in *The Philosophy of Right*. The global economy is also capitalist according to the stricter more technical usage of the term capitalist, especially that of Marx in *Capital*. In the global economy, capital has penetrated production and commodity production prevails. One implication of this is that subjective labour power is separated from the objective conditions of labour. The further implication is that two opposed classes emerge, those who own or control the means of production and those whose only property is their labour power and who are thus compelled to submit to exploitation.

These three points need elaboration. First, the generalization of commodity production. The world has become one vast market and production a moment of exchange. We easily see that this is the case when we consider the role of international trade in the global economy. There is no country in the contemporary world which does not depend heavily on exports and imports. There is no country which is not preoccupied with the balance of payments, with promoting foreign exchange earnings and demand for its exports. National economies have become integrated to the point where a crisis in one economy is rapidly transmitted to others. All these are manifestations of the prevalence of commodity production in the global economy, a development which many writers, including Marx and Engels, foresaw decades ago:

> 'The bourgeoisie has through its exploitation of the world market given a cosmopolitan character to production and consumption in every country. To the great chagrin of Reactionists, it has drawn under the feet of industry the national ground on which it stood. All old-established national industries have been destroyed. They are dislodged by new industries, whose introduction becomes a life and death question for all civilized nations, by industries that no longer work up indigenous raw materials, but raw materials drawn from the remotest zones; industries whose products are consumed, not only at home, but in every quarter of the globe. In place of the old wants, satisfied by the production of the country, we find new wants, requiring for their satisfaction the products of distant lands and climes. In place of the old local and national seclusion and self-sufficiency, we have intercourse in every direction, universal interdependence of nations . . .
>
> The bourgeoisie, by the rapid improvement of all instruments of production, by the immensely facilitated means of communication, draws all, even the most barbarian, nations into civilization. The cheap prices of its commodities are all the heavy artillery with which it batters down all Chinese walls, with which it forces the barbarians' intensely obstinate hatred of foreigners to capitulate. It compels all nations, on pain of extinction, to adopt the bourgeois mode of production; it compels them to introduce what it calls civilization into their midst, i.e. to become bourgeois themselves. In one word, it creates a world after its own image.' [1]

However indifferent or even hostile countries may be to one another, they are now interdependent. This reciprocal economic dependence is in the final analysis the only common interest in the global economy. What Marx said of individuals in capitalist society is applicable to countries in the global economy. Each country's production depends on the production of other countries and the ability of each country to transform what it produces into the means of satisfying its essential needs depends on the consumption of other countries. The pursuit of the private interest of each country now seems inseparable from serving the interests of other countries. What lies behind this appearance is the fact that 'private interest, itself already socially determined' by the international society, is achievable only under the conditions laid down by the international society and by the means which it provides. Countries and groups pursue their private interest 'but its content, as well as the form and means of its realization, is given by social conditions independent of all.' [2]

I now turn to the second aspect of commodity production, namely the separation of the subjective labour process from the objective conditions of labour. My point of departure is Marx's analysis of the labour process, the 'personal activity of man i.e. work itself', the object of that work, and the instruments by which it is done. [3] In the first place, the labour process involves the application of man's faculties to the performance of some task. But the 'labouring' is done on something, and this something is the object of labour. The object of labour is 'all those things which labour merely separates from immediate connection with their immediate environment', [4] for instance all raw materials. Man not only labours on something, but he usually needs something to labour with. That is where the third element of the labour process comes in. The instrument of labour is what man interposes between himself and the objects of labour, what he makes use of to fashion other substances according to his desires. Marx rightly emphasizes the enormous importance of this third element of the labour process. 'It is not the articles made, but how they are made, and by what instruments, that enables us to distinguish different economic epochs. Instruments of labour not only supply a standard of the degree of development to which human labour has attained, but they are also indicators of the social conditions under which that labour is carried on.' [5]

The separation of the subjective labour process from the material conditions of labour is expressed in the buying and selling of labour power. Most people in capitalist society have to sell their labour power, that being the only commodity they have. Others, the capitalists who possess the instruments of labour, buy labour power. Eventually the alienation of the subjective labour process from the material conditions of labour is objectified in the existence of two antagonistic social classes, those who 'have made themselves the owners of the material conditions of labour', and those who, possessing nothing but labour power, 'can only work, and therefore live, with their permission.' [6]

The global capitalist economy also has this characteristic. As in the case of the national capitalist economy, the establishment of the global economy is based on the appropriation of the means of production by the few so that the many no longer have the capability of realizing their own labour. The process by which the few seize the means of production and reduce the many to selling their labour power is primitive accumulation; primitive because it constitutes the prehistory of the capitalist system. Primitive accumulation has already occurred on a world scale. By colonialism and the different forms of imperialism, some countries have deprived others of access to the means of production and thereby created the preconditions of the contemporary capitalist global economy. It is important to add that global primitive accumulation performed a dual function. On the one hand it created the preconditions of global capitalist accumulation. On the other, it created a world economy, that is it integrated a multiplicity of economies into one coherent whole. The core of the integration is the reciprocal dependence of those who own the means of production and those who sell labour power.

Capitalist accumulation, following in the wake of primitive accumulation, has reinforced and accelerated all the processes mentioned above. There is now a neat and radical division of the world into those countries which monopolize the instruments of labour and those which do not possess them. This situation is reflected in the fact that 70% of the population of the world produces only 7% of its industrial output. A few countries have managed to acquire monopoly over the two fundamental instruments of labour in the global capitalist system, namely capital and technology, particularly the latter which is the decisive instrument of production in the world today. The vast majority of countries, especially the Third World countries, lack these instruments of labour and have succumbed to exploitation.

It is necessary to clarify this point. The assertion that some countries do not have the requisite instruments of labour appears to be contradicted by the fact that the Governments of even the poorest of the Third World countries command considerable financial resources and some technology. The idea of countries without instruments of labour also appears to be contradicted by the conventional recognition of national sovereignty over the resources within the national territory. However these contradictions are more apparent than real. National sovereignty over the resources of the national territory is an abstract right for all but a few countries. The reality is that most Third World countries have very limited control over their resources, and as long as they lack the instruments of labour to exploit them, such control would make little difference. The Third World countries are dependent on a few powerful countries for virtually all their technology. They can realize their labour only at the pleasure of the monopolizers of technology and they can transform the objects of labour available to them to the satisfaction of their needs only at the pleasure of these monopolizers of technology. As far as the financial resources of Third World countries, especially African countries, are concerned, they are only slightly less meagre than their technology, certainly not of a magnitude to merit being regarded as a significant means of production. To illustrate, on a very rough estimate most African countries depend on external funds for anything from 50 to 60% or more of their development expenditure. So much for the question of the separation of the subjective labour process from the objective conditions of labour in the global capitalist economy. Let me now turn to the third point, namely the division of the world capitalist economy into two opposed classes.

Classes are functions of production; they emanate from the contradictions within the relations of production which are associated with man's relation to the instruments of labour. More specifically, classes are the social categories arising from the distribution of the agents of production according to their relation to the instruments of labour as owners or non-owners.

In the contemporary world economy it is capital and technology, particularly the latter, which mediate between man and nature; it is by means of these factors that modern man produces, harnesses nature to the satisfaction of his wants. The global production system is divided into those countries which relate to nature as non-owners of capital and technology and those countries which relate to it as owners of capital and technology. This distribution is the class division of the global production system. Henceforth, I shall refer to the two classes as bourgeois and proletarian countries. To avoid confusion, let me emphasize that this classification is based on the countries' shares of the world's capital and technology. So all the highly industrialized countries such as Sweden and Germany are bourgeois countries. More significantly even internally progressive countries such as the Soviet Union must be regarded as bourgeois countries. To classify a country as bourgeois does not mean that it is unprogressive or that its internal economy is capitalist. By the same token when a country is classified as a proletarian country, we are not saying anything about its being progressive in its internal politics, but rather we are saying something about its share of the world's capital and technology. That is not to say that the classification has no political consequences nor even that it does not imply expectations about reactionary or progressive behaviour. It does. Irrespective of the ideology of a country, its place in this classification is a matter of great importance which affects its behaviour and creates contradictions between it and other countries with a similar ideology which are on the other side of the classification. Thus one would expect that the Soviet Union will be less enthusiastic about the redistribution of the world's capital and technology than Mozambique. Similarly, France will be less enthusiastic about such a redistribution than Senegal. So in a sense the Soviet Union and France stand together and struggle against Mozambique and Senegal. Of course, on another level of analysis, the Soviet Union and Mozambique, as progressive countries, stand together and struggle against Senegal and France. Reality is full of contradictions, and we cannot grasp it unless we learn to think dialectically.

Let me return to the two classes of countries. Before proceeding to a discussion of the struggle between these classes I want to draw attention to some concrete indications of their existence. One empirical indicator is the distribution of the instruments of labour, in the present context, technology and capital. There is clearly corroboration on this score. It is not necessary to try to show that the underdeveloped countries have an insignificant share of these instruments of labour. But I ought to point out how this reality presents itself to our consciousness in the form of the distinction we commonly make between industrialized countries and primary producers or suppliers of raw materials. The terminology of this distinction is most revealing. The adjective 'industrial' tells a lot about production and about man's relation to nature. To call a country highly industrialized is to imply that it possesses the advanced technology to transform nature in order to meet its needs. We never say that a technologically backward country is industrialized and we associate industrialization with the possibility of escaping from extreme want, if not with prosperity. The terms 'primary producers' or 'producers of raw materials' imply a completely different relationship with nature. They suggest a certain directness in this relationship, a lack of mediation. Above all, they suggest a lack of technology or at any rate the presence of only a rudimentary technology. Lacking the means to transform nature the proletarian countries can only appropriate it in its rawness if at all.

Another factor indicative, perhaps symptomatic would be more accurate, of the class character of the relation between the developed and the underdeveloped countries is the gap in incomes. The extent of the gap is stunning. For instance, whilst the per capita income of the majority of African countries is under $200, that of the OECD countries is about $4000. The underdeveloped countries' per capita incomes at constant prices would rise from $105 in 1970 to $108 in 1980, an increase of only $3 in 10 years. The comparative figures for the developed countries show an increase from $3100 to $4000 or $900 over the same decade; that is 300 times the increase in the underdeveloped countries.

International politics is increasingly reflecting the importance of the contradiction between the bourgeois and the proletarian countries. As the contradiction has deepened, it has become politicized, and something similar to a class struggle is taking place. One of the more striking manifestations is the attempt to resolve the secondary contradictions within both the bourgeois and proletarian group of countries. This attempt is an important influence on contemporary international politics although it is not recognized for what it is, the consolidation of class forces. Thus the solidaristic movements within the bourgeois countries such as the EEC, NATO and the OECD are represented as the very antithesis of what they are, as contradictions rather than as the resolution of contradiction. The EEC, for example, is said to express the contradiction between the interests of Western Europe on the one hand and those of the United States and the Soviet Union on the other. To represent this alignment as expressing contradictions is strictly speaking not incorrect, but it is somewhat misleading, rather like saying that a difficulty has not been resolved instead of saying that considerable progress has been made towards the resolution of the difficulty. Here the difficulty is the creation of solidarity among the bourgeois countries. To be sure it has not been overcome. Yet considerable progress has been made towards overcoming it, for whatever else it may be, a body such as the EEC represents some transcendence of the contradictions among individual countries of the developed world.

Similar solidaristic tendencies are evident among the proletarian countries. Some examples are the Bandung Afro-Asian Conference in 1955, the Nonaligned Nations Conference in Belgrade in 1961, the 'Group of 77', the Organization of Petroleum Exporting Countries, the Arab League, the Pan African Movement and the Afro-Arab Summit. The distinctive and common economic status of the proletarian countries in the world economy compels attention; the solidarity of these countries which is inevitable though yet unaccomplished is already taken for granted. This is evidenced in the fact that we refer to them as the Third World, 'developing' or less euphemistically, 'underdeveloped' countries.

The political aspect of the struggle between bourgeois and proletarian countries is quite evident in the United Nations. The hegemonic factions of the bourgeois countries, especially the United States, are trying to preserve the present undemocratic structure of the United Nations which allows the hegemonic bourgeois countries to dominate decision-making in the organization. The bourgeois countries, reflecting their class interests, have resisted reform of the organization, and have branded the demand for reforms an irresponsible attempt to destroy it. The proletarian countries for their part reflect their objective interests in demanding democratization of the organization and its use as an instrument against imperialism, racism, neo-colonialism and economic exploitation. Of course the political struggle between the two classes is not limited to the United Nations. The class character of the attempt to resolve the Middle East crisis is obvious. The same can be said of the recent Helsinki Accord and the whole exercise of detente between the US and the USSR, and of the constant attempt by the leaders of the bourgeois countries to install puppet regimes and undermine or destroy militantly anti-imperialist regimes in the proletarian countries. The relation between such policies and the interests of the bourgeois countries, especially the hegemonic factions, does not call for further elaboration.

Each side in this struggle is using an ideology which reflects its interests. Quite naturally the proletarian countries are preoccupied with exploitation, inequality and oppression. The proletarian countries are the champions of change, of a new international economic order. Obviously they are the ones who have nothing to lose by changing the present global production system, and everything to gain. Finally the relation between the condition and consciousness of the proletarian countries is evident in their tendency to see international relations in terms of the concepts of imperialism, neo-colonialism and unequal exchange. The bourgeois countries, for their part, talk of order, peaceful coexistence, peaceful change, stability, responsibility, unity and the struggle between East and West. Most importantly they talk about development.

To all appearances the idea of development is the core concept of the ideology of the bourgeois countries. The bourgeois countries are trying to make the proletarian countries think of their destiny in terms of the possibility of development and the development in question amounts to superficial *embourgeoisement* of the proletarian countries. To the extent that the proletarian countries allow the quest for development to shape their orientations, their revolutionary ardour is curbed, their proletarian solidarity is weakened and their sense of inferiority is reinforced. While propagating the idea of development, the bourgeois countries offer themselves as the guarantors of the possibility of development and proclaim a 'partnership in development'. Assistance is given to make the partnership look plausible but as it is worked out the proletarian countries get poorer and the technological gap widens. Still, the idea of development and the partnership in development creates the illusion of an identity of interest.

On the economic front the struggle has been particularly intense. The proletarian countries have concentrated mainly on joining together to manipulate market forces in order to get more for their raw materials. The most dramatic manifestation of this strategy is the formation of the Organization of Petroleum Exporting Countries. The impact of OPEC and the energy crisis are too well known to detain us here. It is rather more important to note that OPEC is only one of numerous cartels which the proletarian countries have formed as weapons of struggle. The most important of these cartels are as follows. 1. The International Tin Agreement, (Bolivia, Malaysia, Thailand), whose members produce about 80% of the tin of the so called free world. ITA managed to increase the price of tin by 50% in 1973 by cutting supplies by about 20%. 2. The International Council of Copper Exporting Countries (CIPEC). The members of CIPEC are Zaire, Zambia, Chile and Peru. This cartel has not been effective because the United States which is the world's largest producer of copper does not belong to it. Because of the United States boycott, CIPEC controls only about 20% of the world's copper. 3. The Association of Natural Rubber Producing Countries, consisting of Indonesia, Sri Lanka, Singapore, Vietnam, Malaysia and Thailand. This organization controls 90% of the world export market, but it has not been very effective either, for fear of a switch to synthetic substitutes. 4. The International Bauxite Association (IBA) whose members are Guyana, Guinea, Jamaica, Yugoslavia, Surinam, Sierre Leone and Australia. These countries account for about 75% of all aluminium and bauxite exports. IBA has succeeded in increasing revenue from bauxite and aluminium exports, but it is frightened by the possibility of a switch to non-bauxite clays. 5. The Union of Banana Exporting Countries, consisting of Honduras, Colombia, Nicaragua, Guatemala, Panama and Costa Rica. UBEC controls most of the world's banana exports but has been singularly unsuccessful because of the demand elasticity of its product.

Apart from the cartel strategy, the proletarian countries have been striving for more capital, the transfer of technology and the stabilization of export earnings from primary products. These policies are significant only as concrete manifestations of a class struggle which develops the consciousness of the proletarian countries. They have not succeeded and they cannot succeed in rescuing the proletarian countries from wretchedness and oppression. That task cannot be accomplished in a manner compatible with the maintenance of existing relations of production in the world economy. Indeed these policies have not even succeeded in preventing the proletarian countries from falling further behind. For instance, despite the cartel strategy, the price of manufactured goods has risen faster than those of primary exports, and the terms of trade and foreign reserves situation of the proletarian countries have worsened. According to McNamara's 1975 report to the Board of Governors of the World Bank, the price of the exports of the non-oil exporting developing countries rose by 27% in 1974 and very little if any rise was expected for 1975. The comparative figure for their imports is a 40% price increase in 1974 and a projected additional increase of at least 6% in 1975. Despite the incessant pressuring for more aid, there has been no significant capital inflow. An annual average capital inflow of $49 billion would be necessary to sustain an annual increase of 1.2% in per capita income for the poorest countries. The 1974 level of capital inflow was only $34 billion. Even if there was enough capital inflow to sustain a per capita increase of 1.2%, the proletarian countries would still be falling farther behind.

The economic struggle of the bourgeois countries has followed a predictable path. Their general strategy is now clear. On the other hand they want to mitigate the hostility and the revolutionary ardour of the proletarian countries. On the other hand they want to maintain existing relations of production in the global economy. In pursuit of the first part of this strategy, they engage in calculated altruism, hence the 'partnership' in development, the development aid and technical assistance. More recently, the bourgeois countries have expressed some interest in a 'fairer' distribution of the world's wealth and in stabilizing the prices of primary products. The token character of this 'generosity' and its utter insignificance for dealing with the problem of international inequality is easily illustrated. Assume a target per capita income growth of 3.6% in the proletarian countries. This is obviously an extremely modest target, so modest that its achievement would still leave the proletarian countries falling farther behind. The best that one can say is that its achievement will be utterly insignificant as far as bridging the gap between the bourgeois and the proletarian countries is concerned. To achieve this target, capital flows from the bourgeois countries would have to reach 0.7% of the GNP of these countries by 1980. But the capital outflow from the bourgeois countries is presently no more than 0.33% of GNP. What is more, it is declining and expected to fall to about 0.28%. Before leaving this point, one interesting comparison should be made. The World Bank projects that OPEC countries will make available about $4.5 billion in aid to their fellow proletarian countries. This amount represents about 3% of the GNP of the OPEC countries. Comparing volume of aid *as a proportion of GNP*, the ratio of OPEC aid to that of the bourgeois countries is approximately 10:1.

Aid is one of the two fronts on which the bourgeois countries claim to be tackling the problem of inequality in the world. The other is the commodity problem, i.e. the price instability of raw materials and the increase in the price of manufactured goods relative to primary products.

On this front, very little has been achieved beyond the recognition by the bourgeois countries that there is a commodity problem. The United States, which has refused to entertain any interference with market forces, has only just come round to entertaining discussion of price stabilization.

A special session of the General Assembly of the United Nations which opened in September 1975 discussed the problems of development including the price of raw materials. How these good intentions will be implemented is already becoming clear. UNCTAD has prepared a plan to ensure equilibrium between the production and the consumption of primary commodities and to minimize short-run price fluctuations. The proposal calls for the World Bank to furnish a loan for the creation of a buffer stock for particular commodities, which can be supplemented or off-loaded on the market to keep prices within a forecast range; intervention prices are to be fixed by agreement of both producers and consumers. This arrangement can hardly help the primary producers especially since it does not deal with the relation of the prices of primary commodities and manufactured goods. Index-linking which was originally proposed as part of the arrangement was strongly opposed.

To date, the most important attack on the commodity problem is STABEX the scheme for stabilizing export revenues which emerged from the Lome Convention. The scheme involves more primary commodities and more countries than any other one. STABEX is an agreement between the EEC and Africa along the following lines: if the prices of the commodities covered in the agreement fall by 7.5% compared to the average price of the last four years, African countries will be entitled to compensation provided that the decline is due to the free play of market forces. [8] The commodities eligible for compensation are bananas, cotton, coffee, cocoa, coconuts, groundnuts, hides and skins, iron ore, palm and palm kernels, raw sisal, tea and timber. To pay this compensation the EEC has established a fund with a total value of $375 million for 5 years. One fifth of the amount may be paid in compensations for any single year, but, if exceptional circumstances warrant it, an additional 20% may be borrowed from the next year's payment. In effect the maximum compensation payable for any given year is $90 million. The compensation is repayable in good years but this repayment is waived for those countries which came under the category 'least developed countries'. Now, it does not require much analysis to see that this scheme is a token gesture. The maximum compensation payable for each year, $90 million, is utterly insignificant given the large number of African countries and the large number of commodities involved. All minerals are excluded from the scheme except iron ore, even though Africa depends heavily on mineral exports. Crude oil is now Africa's most valuable export; the next most valuable is copper which incidentally is particularly susceptible to price fluctuations. The scheme is unlikely to cost the EEC anything at all , since current prices are likely to be higher than the average prices of the preceding four years due to rising production costs. Finally and most importantly STABEX does not provide compensation for import inflation. [9]

So far I have dealt with only one aspect of the economic struggle of the bourgeois countries, namely the pacification of the proletarian countries. I have suggested that a related aspect of their economic struggle is the preservation of the current inequalities and relations of production in the global system. I will not dwell on this aspect because, as we have seen, the very policies which they have adopted for ameliorating the plight of the proletarian countries fully reveal their determination to preserve the existing order.

The character of the struggle between the proletarian and bourgeois countries allows us to see the global economy in much clearer relief. Perhaps the most striking thing about this struggle is the apparent weakness of the proletarian countries. They are obliged to appeal to charity and to make do with a pittance. They have been manoeuvred into a form of contest in which their defeat is guaranteed; they are fighting for marginal increase in their share of the distribution of the product instead of a redistribution of the capacity to produce. So far the proletarian countries have not been able to back up the pursuit of their interests with force or effective sanctions. The cartel strategy which represents their most forceful policy has merely underlined their weakness, for cartel strategy is failing even in the case of OPEC. Primary producers are under greater pressure to sell their products than the industrialized countries are to buy them. This is due to the fact that primary producers largely have monocultural export economies, and to the elasticity of supply of primary products. The limited success in raising prices has merely redistributed purchasing power in favour of the bourgeois countries. To begin with, the majority of proletarian countries which do not produce oil suffered even more severely from rising oil prices than did the bourgeois countries. The bourgeois countries were able to foist part of their oil bill onto the proletarian countries by increasing the price of manufactured goods. Finally, because of the internal class contradictions in most of the OPEC countries such as Iran and Saudi Arabia, a good portion of the petrodollars find their way back to the bourgeois countries. In *The Control of Oil* Professor Blair meticulously deploys evidence to show that the big international oil companies, such as Exxon, Shell and Standard Oil of New Jersey, benefitted more from OPEC's cartel strategy than anyone else. He also shows that the OPEC countries have no really significant power of coercion, that the big oil companies could easily defeat OPEC by their control of technology and marketing.

The failures of the proletarian countries reflect their lack of instruments of labour. It is because they lack instruments of labour that the proletarian countries are unable to use their objects of labour as an effective weapon in the economic struggle. It is for this reason that even OPEC is weak. To get oil in the first place OPEC depends entirely on the technology of the bourgeois countries. Because the bourgeois countries monopolize the instruments of labour, they are able to redeem the petrodollars and to pass on the burden of OPEC's price hike to the proletarian countries as import inflation. Quite clearly, the economic struggle of the rich and poor countries underlines the radical division of the world into countries which monopolize the instruments of labour and those who possess no instruments of labour. This analysis suggests that the proletarian countries are neither likely nor able to overcome their poverty or to prevent themselves from falling farther behind. I will now turn to the relation of the global struggle to the internal situation in Africa.

THE GLOBAL STRUGGLE AND THE AFRICAN SITUATION

There is no reason to believe that the global class struggle will culminate in a global revolution, that is a revolutionary overthrow of the power of bourgeois countries by proletarian countries, in the foreseeable future. This is so mainly because of the class contradiction within the proletarian countries. With few exceptions, such as Vietnam, Cuba, and Guinea Bissau, the ruling classes of the proletarian countries cannot mobilize their people for a proletarian revolution against the bourgeois countries because of the contradictions between them and the masses of their country, and because of the links between them and the ruling class of the bourgeois countries. Like the ruling classes of the bourgeois countries their interests are ultimately opposed to a proletarian revolution, be it on the national or the global level. Nevertheless, they must act out the necessities of the contradiction between the bourgeois countries and the proletarian countries; they must accomodate and to some extent express the revolutionary impulses inherent in the situation of the proletarian countries. However, they will tend to express these impulses tamely, as petty-bourgeois radicalism or as nationalism. In short the global struggle cannot culminate in a global revolution unless particular proletarian countries universalize the condition of the proletariat internally, that is undergo socialist revolutions.

What is interesting about the global class struggle is not so much that it tells us about the prospects of global revolution, but that it sheds light on class contradictions and revolutionary pressures in specific countries. For the rest of this chapter I will consider the effects of the global struggle on Africa.

My thesis is that the global struggle will exacerbate and radicalize the major contradiction in the relations of production of the African nations, the contradiction between the African bourgeoisie and the African proletariat, and by so doing hasten and effect its resolution in the form of a socialist revolution. The global class struggle has two kinds of effects on Africa: (a) it develops material conditions favourable to revolution;

(b) it develops a political consciousness favourable to revolution.

Let us consider the first type of effect. To avoid confusion, I should begin by noting that the 'material conditions favourable to revolution' in Africa and other parts of the proletarian world were not created by the global class struggle. They were brought into being by the very factor which also created the conditions of the global struggle. The factor in question is global primitive accumulation and its determinate forms in Africa were imperialism and colonialism. Imperialism and colonialism expropriated Africa and made it a capitalist economy with a particularly sharp contradiction between the bourgeoisie and the proletariat despite the rudimentary development of the forces of production. What the global class struggle is doing is merely to further the development of conditions which the process of global primitive accumulation had already created.

The expropriation of Africa, and the unequal exchange between Africa and the bourgeois nations which arose from it, have kept Africa pitifully underdeveloped. The global class struggle is pushing Africa nearer to revolution by exacerbating some of the consequences of Africa's under-development. To be specific, the global class struggle will make Africa lag farther behind the bourgeois countries and perpetuate her desperate poverty in an increasingly affluent world.

In order to protect their own interest in the face of the developing class struggle, the bourgeois countries are taking steps to make themselves less vulnerable to the pressure of the proletarian countries. Given the circumstances of the global class struggle, there are two major ways in which they can do this. One is to make themselves less dependent on raw materials from the proletarian countries. I will not dwell on this rather obvious point; in any case, it has already been mentioned. However, I ought to note that Africa will suffer greatly from the bourgeois countries' drive for self-sufficiency in raw materials. One reason is that the bulk of her raw material exports is in non-essential raw materials such as ground-nuts, cocoa, coffee, cotton, palm oil, sisal, hides and skins. Copper, which is Africa's most valuable export after oil, is a mineral for which substitutes are easily found. Another reason is that the drive for self sufficiency will be directed primarily against the poorest and most exploited members of the proletarian world who have also become the most radical opponents of the existing property relations in the world economy. As the bourgeois nations reduce their dependence on raw materials it will be more difficult for Africa to prevent herself from sinking into more desperate poverty.

Self-sufficiency in raw materials is really a secondary line of defence for the bourgeois nations. Their primary line of defence must be to increase or at least maintain their technological dominance. As we have seen, technology is the crucial instrument of labour in the world economy. The distribution of technology determines all the major distributions and divisions in the world economy. It determines who can realize their labour and who must sell their labour power within the global class system. It determines the division of labour and the distribution of the product. And we must not forget that technology is perhaps the most important determinant of the ability of the bourgeois countries to do without the raw materials of the proletarian countries, since technology facilitates the manipulation of production inputs and processes. Finally, the military supremacy of the bourgeois nations depends almost entirely on their technology.

Because technology is so crucial in these ways, the bourgeois countries try hard to advance their technology and to limit technological transfer to the proletarian countries as the global class struggle grows in intensity. There is every indication that their technological dominance will continue to increase. For instance, many studies indicate that, for the world as a whole, the control of technology is becoming more concentrated as technology advances. [10] We may thus reasonably conjecture that the technological gap will increase despite all the talk about the transfer of technology. The question is how will this development, that is the widening of the technological gap, affect Africa. It will have the effect of rendering Africa even more defenceless against exploitation and even more incapable of overcoming her desperate poverty. The development in question underpins Africa's relegation to the role of an agent of production which can produce and so live only by the permission of others. Not only is Africa relegated to the role of selling labour power, the utility of this labour power is being diminished. The advancement of technology increases productivity and reduces unit costs of production. However, because of the peculiarities of the international market, the bourgeois countries are able to monopolize the benefits of the cheapness of manufactured goods made possible by technological progress. Indicative of this is the tendency for the rise in the price of primary products from the proletarian countries to lag far behind the rise of the price in manufactured goods consumed by the proletarian nations. For example, for the two decades ending about 1974, the price of primary products was virtually stagnant while the price of manufactured goods increased at the startling rate of about 10% per annum.

The effects of the global struggle on the relation between the ruling classes of African countries and those of the bourgeois countries are very important. Against the background of economic and technological dependence of African countries, we may call this relation a patron-client relation. There are many contradictions in this relation. These contradictions are connected and may be treated collectively as one major contradiction; the one between political power and economic power. The African ruling class is the political power while the ruling class of the bourgeois countries is the economic power. The reality of economic dependence limits the political power of the African ruling class, while the reality of the political power of the African ruling class may to some extent limit the economic power of the ruling class of the bourgeois countries to manipulate and exploit Africa. The limitations frustrate both sides, and the parties involved strive to overcome them. So, despite the fact that the interests of the African ruling class and those of its patrons in the bourgeois countries coincide in some respects, the two classes are also in struggle.

How does the global struggle between proletarian and bourgeois countries affect this struggle between client and patron ruling classes? To begin with, the ruling class of an African country has a dual role: as a comprador bourgeoisie acting as the puppet protecting the interests of the ruling class of the bourgeois countries, and secondly as the political governor of the proletariat within an African country. In order to maintain its rule, the African ruling class must give expression to the revolutionary pressures arising from the existential conditions of its subjects. Since it is in the interest of this class to ameliorate the desperate poverty of its subjects, it must fight to accelerate economic growth, if not economic development, at home and to gain control over a greater share of the world's resources. But insofar as acceleration of economic growth depends on ending exploitative relations with bourgeois countries and transforming the global economic structure to improve the chances of proletarian countries, this aspiration will generate conflict between client and patron classes. Efforts to increase African countries' share of the world's resources will have the same effect. As the global class struggle develops and the contradictions between bourgeois and proletarian countries deepen, the ruling classes of the latter will be obliged to make such efforts even more strenuously and the mutual alienation of client and patron classes will increase accordingly.

That is only one side of the coin. The ruling classes of the bourgeois countries are also obliged to reinforce this alienation. For the most part, the policies which they have to pursue to protect their own interests as the global struggle intensifies will be inimical to the interests of their African clients. For instance, consider the two lines of defence of the bourgeois countries which we have mentioned, the quest for self-sufficiency in industrial raw materials and the widening of the technological gap. As we have seen, if these policies are at all successful they threaten Africa with economic stagnation or decline into even greater poverty. Such a development is clearly not in the interest of the African ruling classes; economic stagnation will erode their veneer of legitimacy and hasten their revolutionary liquidation.

What is the significance of this evolving contradiction between the patron and client ruling classes? One consequence is that the development of the forces of production in Africa will be retarded even as capitalist exploitation proceeds apace. The contradiction increases the uncertainties and risks of the bourgeois countries' economic exploitation of Africa. It is unclear how their fear (associated with increasing uncertainty and risk) and their greed will find equilibrium. However the most probable effect of this contradiction on the bourgeois countries' calculations is quite clear.

It will decrease their inclination to invest in Africa. They will be particularly averse to investment involving a long gestation period. Rather they will invest mainly for quick returns and in more mobile assets which can be rescued on short notice. We have to expect that in Africa the organic composition of capital will increase very little, if at all, and that surplus value extracted from African labour will tend to be exported rather than transformed into capital in Africa. This greatly worsens Africa's prospect of avoiding economic stagnation and overcoming poverty.

Another consequence of this developing contradiction is that it will compel the African ruling class to be more independent economically, for instance it will have to make more serious efforts to mobilize capital internally for financing its development and recurrent expenditure. One effect of such independence would be that the exploitative character and the failings of the African ruling class will be revealed more clearly. For instance if there is less aid from abroad, then it will become that much more difficult to temper the harshness of underdevelopment; as more and more demands are made on the people, questions about the equitable sharing of the burdens and the rewards of the system will compel attention. Perhaps the most positive thing about this enforced independence is that it makes some contribution to the radicalization of the consciousness of the African proletariat. Beyond this it does not really help to overcome underdevelopment; in so far as it intensifies exploitation of the African masses, it actually reinforces it.

The global class struggle will lead to an effort to reduce the contradictions within each bourgeois country, particularly the contradiction between bourgeoisie and proletariat. We must assume this because the bourgeoisie of the bourgeois countries have a strong interest in reducing, or hiding, this contradiction. This is so because they will be less capable of dealing with the pressures from the proletarian countries if their own house is divided. They must also contain the pressures from the proletarian countries in order to preserve a production system that serves them so well. As this bourgeoisie divert resources to the amelioration of conditions at home, they have less to give towards the amelioration of conditions in the proletarian countries. A related point is that to paper over the basic internal contradiction of the bourgeois countries, the bourgeoisie of these countries have to play up the antagonism of the proletarian countries towards the bourgeois countries. In doing this they undermine the legitimacy of putting resources into the amelioration of conditions in the proletarian countries. Finally the promotion by this bourgeoisie of antagonistic feelings towards the proletariat of the proletarian countries will weaken international proletarian solidarity and hence Africa's ability to extract concessions from the bourgeois countries. These developments do not augur well for Africa's fight against economic stagnation and poverty.

To sum up, the global class struggle is likely to lessen Africa's prospects of overcoming economic stagnation or mollifying the harshness of her poverty. In so far as the global class struggle has these effects, it becomes a powerful agent of revolutionary change in Africa. These effects impose a very severe strain on the maintenance of the relations of production in contemporary Africa. Economic stagnation and desperate poverty deprive the ruling classes of Africa of the chance of maintaining even a veneer of legitimacy. They reveal capitalism in all its grotesqueness and wickedness and compel attention to the necessity of equitable distribution. In short, they amount to strong revolutionary pressures. Against the rising tide of these revolutionary pressures, Africa's ruling classes are quite helpless. They cannot overcome the stagnation and poverty as long as the global production system remains and as long as they maintain the existing property relations in Africa. They will try to deal with the revolutionary impulse largely by repression. But this only radicalizes the internal contradictions.

REVOLUTIONARY POLITICAL CONSCIOUSNESS

As we have seen, the global class struggle aids the development of revolutionary consciousness in Africa indirectly by its influence on the economic condition of Africa. The global struggle also directly determines the development of revolutionary consciousness in Africa. It does this in two major ways: (a) by fostering the ideology of development and (b) by forcing the African ruling classes to adopt a radical ideology.

I will consider the ideology of development first. The dominance of the bourgeois countries in the global struggle is associated with a hegemonic ideology. The dominant ideology in the world today is the ideology of development. It is this ideology which reflects the consciousness and rationalizes the interests of the dominant class, the bourgeois countries. The ideology of development views world history as a process of development. The degree of development supposedly determines all the essential capabilities of a nation-state including the capability for democracy, political stability, overcoming poverty, etc. According to this ideology, development has been achieved in the bourgeois countries; this is apparently not incompatible with the admission that some development is still occurring in these countries. In the rest of the world, however, development is largely a promise which is being realized. These countries are still in transition through stages which the developed countries have already gone through. Since the characteristics which constitute development are also the salient features of the developed countries, development amounts to becoming more and more like the bourgeois countries.

How this ideology rationalizes the interests of the bourgeois countries is evident. It encourages admiration and imitation of the bourgeois countries. It reinforces the subordination of the proletarian countries not only by inculcating a sense of inferiority but also by exciting their passion for 'goods' whose supply is controlled by the bourgeois countries. Finally, it misrepresents the cause of the underdevelopment of the proletarian countries by implying that the state of being of the proletarian countries is analgous to that of the bourgeois countries at an earlier stage of their historical evolution.

The bourgeois countries cannot help using an ideology of this sort. And yet the use of this ideology carries a contradiction because it furthers the development of revolutionary consciousness or, at any rate, of strong antipathies towards the property relations of the world economy. Quite simply the promise of development cannot be realized in the context of the present global production system and in the context of the existing system of property relations in Africa. Performance will lag far behind the expectation of development, revealing ever more clearly how the maintenance of the present global production system offers nothing but bondage and wretchedness to Africa and the other proletarian countries. But the poor performance will appear most immediately to the African masses as a failure of their own leaders, and their resentment will accordingly focus on this ruling class.

The second way in which the global class struggle directly fosters the development of radical political consciousness in Africa is by compelling the African ruling classes to adopt a 'progressive' ideology. As we have seen, the global struggle reveals and deepens the contradictions between the African ruling classes and the ruling classes of bourgeois countries. The pertinent point here is how the African ruling class copes with this contradiction. In the most general terms, it will cope with it by maximizing its capacity to put pressure on its patrons; this implies building an independent power base. *Ex hypothesi*, the economic power of the African ruling classes is insignificant. The major weapon at their disposal is their political power over the African masses, and this is the weapon they must use to put pressure on the bourgeois countries. To make this weapon potent, they must promote mass awareness of the contradictions between the proletarian and bourgois countries. An ideology which promotes this awareness is, *ipso facto*, progressive.

Before going into the content of such an ideology, I should mention a related factor which determines the ideology that the African ruling classes must use. The African ruling classes have to cope with the developing contradiction between the bourgeois countries and the proletarian countries. As the global class struggle develops, it becomes increasingly difficult for the African ruling classes to play their client role, it becomes more difficult for them to survive without championing the cause of the proletarian countries or at least making an elaborate show of doing so. In so far as they champion this cause or even make a show of doing so, they must propagate a progressive ideology.

But what will be the content of this ideology? What kind of ideology will promote mass consciousness of the contradiction between the bourgeois and proletarian countries as well as reflect the interest of the proletarian countries? Whatever else it may contain, such an ideology has to be phrased in terms of inequality, exploitation, a struggle between the haves and the have-nots. It must unequivocally uphold the justice of the claims of the have-nots, and condemn inequality and exploitation. That African leaders use an ideology of this nature is already familiar knowledge. Their demand for 'a new international economic order' and their explanations of underdevelopment are made in these terms. In having to resort to such an ideology, Africa's rulers find themselves in the unpleasant situation of digging their own graves. For the values of such an ideology are antithetical to the maintenance of existing relations of production in Africa.

To sum up: in the contemporary world economy, countries (as agents of production) are divided into those who possess instruments of labour and those who essentially possess only labour power. Corresponding to this distribution of the instruments of labour is the division of the world into two classes, (proletarian countries and bourgeois countries), who are engaged in a struggle of ever increasing intensity. As a result of this struggle, strong impetus is being given to the development of revolutionary pressures in Africa. To all appearances this development is irreversible.

NEO - COLONIAL DEPENDENCE

In Chapter 1, I looked at Africa in the global context and tried to trace in outline the revolutionary pressures arising from the dynamics of Africa's situation in the global system. In the present chapter, I want to focus on only one salient feature of Africa's situation in the global system, namely neo-colonial dependence. Analysis of neo-colonial dependence illustrates the enormous influence of international social forces on the internal situation in African countries, particularly in developing revolutionary pressures. I will concentrate on showing how examination of neo-colonial dependence sheds light on the necessity and the probability of socialist revolutions in Africa. I will be taking for granted the causal relation of neo-colonial dependence to the underdevelopment of Africa; several well-known studies have treated this subject exhaustively and competently. Some examples of these studies are A.G. Frank, *Capitalism and Under-development in Latin America*; Walter Rodney, *How Europe Under-developed Africa*; Samir Amin, *Accumulation on a World Scale*; A. Emmanuel, *Unequal Exchange: A Study of the Imperialism of Trade*; Colin Leys, *Kenya: The Political Economy of Neocolonialism*; Tomas Szentes, *The Political Economy of Underdevelopment*. Since the consequences of neo-colonial dependence are fairly clear, I will concentrate on the problem of indigenizing [1] African economies, that is to say the problem of extricating Africa from neo-colonial dependence.

NEO-COLONIALISM AND THE AFRICAN BOURGEOISIE

The Argument

Neo-colonial dependence is of course the effect of imperialism, which integrated Africa into the world capitalist system. From this premise it is easy to proceed to the inference that the elimination or reduction of neo-colonial dependence is merely a matter of fighting imperialism without necessarily confronting the internal ruling class. This line of reasoning is quite misleading. But, unfortunately, it is quite current. African leaders have encouraged it, perhaps because it serves their interest. It will soon be clear why it is misleading and how it serves the interests of the African bourgeoisie.

I will explore the theme of this chapter in the context of the following thesis: the core of the problem of indigenizing African economies is the contradiction between the bourgeoisie and the proletariat in Africa. The necessary though by no means sufficient condition for solving this problem is the resolution of this contradiction. The African bourgeoisie will carry out only *limited* indigenization calculated to legitimize their rule and to consolidate their class domination. By failing to indigenize their economies completely, the African bourgeoisie digs its own grave, for neo-colonial dependence is at the very root of the economic exploitation and economic stagnation of Africa, the very factors which are generating strong revolutionary pressures in Africa. Thus the problem of indigenization clearly reveals the desirability and inevitability of revolution in Africa. To solve it the African bourgeoisie must destroy capitalism itself, thereby committing suicide as a class. Not to solve it, is to foster the conditions for their revolutionary liquidation.

To develop this thesis, it is desirable to concentrate on two salient features, namely the objective interest and character of the African bourgeoisie and the relation of this bourgeoisie to its subjects.

African Bourgeoisies and Their Weaknesses

The African bourgeoisie suffers from many weaknesses largely associated with the colonial legacy. One of its most significant weaknesses is the lack of a strong material base. Kenya's colonial experience illustrates the point very well. Under colonialism, Kenyans were denied access to wealth. The most productive land in Kenya was reserved for the white settlers. A combination of legal sanctions forced Africans out of these lands. Even though Europeans were less than 1% of the population of Kenya by 1937 while Africans constituted about 98%, nearly the same amount of land was reserved for European use as for African use. Europeans had about 29.5 million acres while Africans had about 31 million acres. Worse still, the land reserved for European use included about 80% of the productive land in Kenya. Africans were effectively barred from engaging in the more profitable types of farming. They were prevented from growing pyrethrum on the excuse of protecting the crop from disease. The Coffee Plantations Registration Ordinance of 1918 prevented Africans from growing coffee. Another law, the Marketing of Native Produce Ordinance of 1935, limited marketing (particularly wholesale trade) to Europeans and Asians. Under this law, Europeans and Asians could prevent Africans from growing any cash crop commercially by simply refusing to buy the crop from them. The Kenyan Africans also suffered crippling credit restrictions. The Credit to Africans Ordinance of 1948 stipulated that debts of over 200 shillings incurred by Africans could not be enforced in court. As a result of this law, credit institutions were unwilling to grant substantial loans to African entrepreneurs.

Policies such as these produced, in post-colonial Africa, a numerically small bourgeoisie with a very weak material base. The point is simply illustrated in Kenya, which is reputedly one of the more prosperous countries in Africa and one of the countries in which the bourgeoisie is most developed. When the ILO Mission made an estimate of household income distribution by economic group and income size in Kenya for 1968-70, it found that only 30,000 households in Kenya, (a country of about 13 million people), earn £1000 sterling and over. The economic group which constitutes this income category consists of 'owners of medium-sized to large non-agricultural enterprises in the formal sector of commerce, industry and services; rentiers; big farmers; self-employed professional people; holders of high-level jobs in the formal sector'. [2] Now the 30,000 households must include a good proportion of Europeans and non-citizen Asians. When we make allowances for this we see that the number of Kenyans in this category is very small as a proportion of the population of Kenya.

Even then, this is not the major aspect of the weakness of the material base of the African bourgeoisie. The major aspect is the dependence of African economies. In the process of integrating Africa into the capitalist system, colonialism turned Africa into an aggregation of monocultural export economies. The capitalist West constitutes the monopoly consumer of African primary products, the monopoly supplier of technology to Africa and the monopoly supplier of loans and grants. To illustrate, Western Europe, Canada and the US accounted for 64.5% of Kenya's total export earnings in 1965, 60.4% in 1970 and 58.7% in 1973. The comparative figures for the communist states (Eastern Europe, the USSR, and China) were 3.5% in 1965, 3.6% in 1970 and 4.3% in 1973. On the import side, the picture is much the same. The share of Western Europe, the US and Canada in Kenya's import expenditure was 59.7% in 1965, 63.3% in 1970, and 62.9% in 1973. By contrast the share of Eastern Europe and China was 3.2% in 1965, 3.3% in 1970 and 3.4% in 1973. [3] By my calculations, based on GATT and UN trade statistics, this trend holds for Africa as a whole. [4] The industrialized capitalist countries' share of the total dollar values of Africa's exports in 1965 was 78.19%; it was 78.73% in 1970 and 75.23% in 1973. By contrast the comparative shares of the communist bloc were 7.35% in 1965, 7.02% in 1970 and 8.45% in 1973. Africa's import statistics tell the same story. The industrialized capitalist countries' share of the total money value of Africa's imports was 71.48% in 1965, 70.41% in 1970 and 72.54% in 1973. Again the communist bloc's share was relatively much smaller; 8.79% in 1965, 10.45% in 1970 and 8.50% in 1973. There are other types of dependence which are just as important, for instance the financial dependence and technological dependence of African countries on the capitalist countries is of a magnitude comparable to their commercial dependence. Obviously the

African bourgeoisie is in the weak and uncomfortable position of governing with only marginal control of its economy.

The African bourgeoisie is not only weak in the sense that I have described above, but its survival is imperilled by strong revolutionary pressures from the African proletariat. These pressures arise from the following circumstances. First, the economic surplus in Africa is particularly small. There is no need to dwell once more on the unhappy statistics of wretchedness and starvation in Africa, but it helps the appreciation of the poverty in Africa to put the matter in comparative perspective. Professor Onitiri has done so with poignant simplicity:

> 'Thus, after a decade of independence, 34 countries of Developing Africa, accounting for about 94% of total population in the area, still record incomes per head of less than $200 per annum. This pitifully low level of economic performance is brought out even more dramatically when comparisons are made with other countries. The total GNP for the forty-four developing countries of Africa is less than that for the Benelux countries, while that of fourteen countries of the West African sub-region is less than the GNP of Turkey. The total GNP of the eight countries of Central Africa is less than that of Peru, while that of the sixteen countries in East Africa is less than that of Finland and only just equal to that of Norway.
>
> More startling results are revealed when comparison is made in the different economic sectors. For example the total imports of West Africa (fourteen countries) are less than those of Mexico, while imports into the sixteen countries of East Africa are at about the same level.' [5]

It remains to add that the economic outlook in Africa has become even more desperate in recent years. The decline in the price of primary products, the rise in the price of imported goods, much higher oil bills, imported inflation, these factors have drastically reduced the rate of growth. Meanwhile protracted drought in several regions in Africa, threatening millions of people with death by starvation, has immensely increased the pressure on existing resources.

The significant point is that all this wretchedness and desperate poverty exists in the context of a highly developed political consciousness among the masses. The African masses were intensely politicized by the nationalist movements. To gain power, the nationalist bourgeoisie had to mobilize the African population behind them. In the circumstances of the colonial situation, this mobilization entailed substantial radicalization. Inevitably the nationalist bourgeoisie had to adopt a political style and a political ideology which would negate the claims of the colonizers. Thus they tried to rehabilitate the self-respect of the Africans and to denigrate colonialism, and they denigrated colonialism by revealing its oppressive and exploitative nature. Against the colonizer's claim to rule, the nationalist leaders asserted the right of self-determination, the inalienable right to freedom and the equality of all men. It is clear therefore that the ideology by which the

African masses were mobilized into politics also radicalized them. It radicalized them by teaching them to value equality and political participation, by sensitizing them to exploitation, by teaching them to resent it and to make it a crucial issue of politics. In using this ideology, the nationalist leaders were involved in a classic contradiction. They could not do without this ideology given their aspiration to overthrow colonialism and come to power. On the other hand, they could not really afford to use this ideology because it was ultimately incompatible with the relations of production which they wanted to maintain.

This contradiction was temporarily submerged by nationalist politics which concentrated on ousting the colonizers. However, when independence came, the contradictions surfaced, and they are now putting the bourgeois regimes of Africa under severe pressure. The new rulers must now bear the brunt of the masses' demand for material betterment, for equality and the end of exploitation. But they cannot meet these demands in a manner compatible with the maintenance of existing relations of production. Since the worsening economic situation leaves them virtually no scope for manoeuvre, they have had to resort increasingly to containing these mass demands by repression. In most of Africa the hegemonic factions of the bourgeoisie have resorted to political violence of a scale and kind that virtually amounts to fascism. While this massive political violence has enabled the bourgeoisie to hang on, it is at the same time deepening and radicalizing the contradictions between them and the masses. As politics increasingly degenerates into warfare, the survival of the bourgeoisie grows ever more problematic and becomes the consuming passion of the bourgeoisie. This is the political background against which Africa is pursuing indigenization.

In these circumstances it is to be expected that the indigenization of African economies will be pursued mainly insofar as it furthers the consolidation of the power of Africa's fledgling bourgeoisie, and promotes the maintenance of existing relations of production. But if existing relations of production are to be maintained, especially when they are capitalist, then there is really no indigenization. The maintenance of the existing capitalist relations of production is incompatible with indigenization. Just as we cannot talk of the dependence and underdevelopment of Africa as something structurally different from the syndrome of imperialism, we cannot dissociate the African bourgeoisie from this syndrome. The African bourgeoisie is as much a mechanism of imperialism as international capital; it is itself a social manifestation of imperialist penetration of Africa; it is in every sense a creation of this penetration and an integral part of the structure of dependence. If the indigenization of African economies is problematic it is partly because the African bourgeoise has fundamental vested interests in the exploitative relations of production which are integral to the structure of dependence, despite the existence of contradictions between it and the metropolitan bourgeoisie. The main priority

for the indigenization of African economies is the liberation of Africa
from the African bourgeoisie, since African societies cannot fight imperialism under the leadership of agents of imperialism. Let us be quite clear
why this is so. The indigenization of African economies must entail their
disengagement from exploitative relations with international capitalism;
this indeed is why indigenization is so important. Therefore, if indigenization is to be anything more than a token gesture, it will jeopardize
the interests of international capitalism. This means that indigenization
must eventually come down to a battle against international capitalism.
And that is the rub. Is the African bourgeoisie in a position to put strong
pressures on Western capitalism? Clearly not. The extent of the financial,
commercial and technological dependence of their economies on the West
does not allow them the requisite leverage. Moreover, the contradictions
which have emerged from the existing relations of production have driven
the African bourgeoisie to seek allies abroad in their battle against their
own people. The ability of the African bourgeoisie to liberate the African
economy is in question. Also at issue is their willingness. In undertaking
such liberation, they would be destroying a major foundation of their
power. More than that, a serious effort at indigenization will greatly
intensify the pressures against the survival of their regime. This is so for
the following reasons. First, international capitalism will throw its weight
against them — and it can marshall more resources to fight its cause than
Africa's corrupt oligarchies. Second, an attempt to disengage African
economies from their crippling dependence will create grave economic
hardships in the short run as the economies readjust and absorb the
sanctions which the Western powers are bound to invoke. The resulting
temporary disequilibrium and the shrinking economic surplus will give
the African bourgeoisie even less room to manoeuvre and will immensely
compound their problems of survival. In these circumstances, indigenization
cannot go very far; the process of indigenization will merely reflect the
overriding interest of the African bourgeoisie in maintaining the existing
relations of production in the face of the strong revolutionary pressures
facing them.

That is my theory. In what follows, I examine the efforts of indigenization in Kenya, Nigeria and Tanzania in order to show that the African
bourgeoisie does not and cannot seriously pursue indigenization beyond
the token measures which consolidate its power and help it in its
competition with the metropolitan bourgeoisie.

CASE STUDIES IN INDIGENIZATION

Kenyan Indigenization: Creation of a Bourgeoisie

The policy for the indigenization of the agricultural sector in Kenya was

initiated before Kenya became independent, and post-independence
Kenya has followed the logic of this policy. Under this policy indigenization was essentially the process of creating an indigenous bourgeoisie
and of transforming a colonial economy into a neo-colonial one.

The indigenization of agriculture in Kenya came down to the question
of transferring the farms and land reserved for Europeans to Africans.
Before independence about 3 million hectares, nearly 80% of the best land
in Kenya, was reserved exclusively for Europeans. This land was divided
into two functional categories. Approximately 1.4 million hectares was
earmarked for mixed farms and about 1.6 million hectares was for use as
plantations for the vital cash crops, sisal, tea, coffee, etc., as well as for
dairy farming. When land hunger in Kenya became manifest with the
Mau Mau insurrection, it became inexpedient for the Europeans to
continue to monopolize the land and the Colonial Government began to
explore the possibility of mitigating land hunger and of giving Africans
greater participation in the agricultural economy in a manner compatible
with the pursuit of their imperialist interests. In January 1961, a scheme
was launched for the settlement of Africans on the white farm lands. The
project was called the Million Acre Settlement Scheme. Under this scheme,
Africans were to be settled on relatively large farms averaging 12 hectares
in size. The scheme also included settlement of Africans on very large
cooperative farms and ranches. It was projected that these larger farms
would involve a land area of 72,000 hectares and provide a living for
about 1,700 farmers. The average cost of establishing each farm under the
Million Acre Settlement Scheme was over K£700.

On the whole the project went very well. According to the Kenyan
Government, 32,000 families had been settled under the scheme on some
400,000 hectares of land by mid 1968. By 1970 the Government met its
target: 35,401 families had been settled under the scheme on some
500,000 hectares of land. To complement the Million Acre Settlement
Scheme, another settlement scheme was launched in 1965. This was
called the Squatter Settlement Programme. It was a much less ambitious
scheme involving less land, fewer families and lower costs. The average
size of the farms under the scheme was only 4.5 hectares. By mid 1968
approximately 13,000 families had been settled under the programme and
by 1970 18,000 families had been settled. [6] This scheme involved less than
100,000 hectares. There was a third important settlement scheme, which
involved the takeover of 1,200 very large farms by individual Africans
and by groups of Africans. The land area involved in this scheme was very
large, about 400,000 hectares. These farms were purchased largely by loans
provided by the Agricultural Finance Corporation (AFC) and the
Agricultural Development Corporation (ADC). All told, about 900,000
hectares or about 60% of the former European farms were transferred to
Africans under these various resettlement schemes. If we take account of
all the settlement schemes and Government land acquisition, including

some minor ones not mentioned here, we get a total settlement area of about 1.5 million acres.

All this seems very impressive. But we have to remember that all the indigenized land under these schemes amounts to only 20% of the total area of the old white highlands. The 1.6 million hectares outside the mixed farm areas, used by the European settlers for raising cash crops such as tea, coffee, sisal and for ranching, were virtually unaffected. The Government of Kenya did not foresee any change in this situation. The 1970-74 *Development Plan* explains the problems as follows:

> 'To purchase a ranch or a plantation as an unit intact normally requires a substantial investment. Very few individual Africans have been able to raise this much capital. Although Africans could obtain the necessary capital more easily if they joined forces with others and formed a partnership, a company or a co-operative society, the amount of capital required by each person is still high and few ranches or plantations have been acquired in this way. Furthermore, neither the ranches nor the plantations are very suitable for sub-division into small-scale farms. During the plan period the same conditions which have previously hindered rapid Africanization of the ranches and plantations will continue to prevail. For this reason it is expected that only a small proportion of the ranches and plantations will be acquired by Africans in the next ten years.' [7]

The land settlement scheme amply reflects the weakness of Kenya's bourgeoisie in relation to their patrons. To begin with, the British insisted and got Kenyan leaders to agree that Africans must pay the full market value of whatever European land was transferred to them. By buying the land at current market prices, Africans were paying exorbitant prices for assets that had originally belonged to them and whose value was increased by a series of malpractices and discriminatory measures. For instance, the value of the land reflected two decades of land speculation by Europeans. The prices paid for the resettled land also reflected the improvements made by the European farmers, but their ability to make these improvements and to prosper depended on the monopolies, (e.g. marketing), extension services and price control which their political influence secured for them. Their contribution to the improvement of the land was made possible by profits associated with their privileges and derived from exploitation of African labour.

All the same, the Africans agreed to pay for the settlement land and the payment became an enormous financial burden to the Government. In the financial year 1963/64 about 75% of all agricultural development expenditure went to the settlement schemes. By the financial year 1968/69, it had fallen somewhat below 50%. [8] Of course, not all the expenditure went in payments to European farmers; some of it went to meet the administrative cost of land transfer. But data on the payments to the European farmers exist: Africans had paid about K£20 million for the 1.5 million acres of land they had reclaimed from the European farmers by 1970.

Let us look more closely at the terms of the land transfer. We shall focus on the Million Acre Scheme which was by far the most ambitious project. As we have seen, the British insisted that the new owners of the farms pay the full market value. This condition was a difficult one because Africans, denied access to wealth under the Colonial Government, could not raise the capital to buy the farms. The British Government then offered to give a sizeable proportion of the capital needed to purchase the European farms and encouraged the Kenyan Government to raise loans from other capitalist countries to make the settlement scheme possible. The finance for the Million Acres Settlement Scheme (£25 million spent by mid 1968) breaks down as follows: £11.3 million in loans received from Western countries and agencies, £9.7 million from the UK and £3.6 million from the Government of Kenya. The foreign loans went to the Government which in turn loaned them to the farmers. The significance of these loans should be clear; they enabled the British Government and imperialist interests to defeat the purposes of the indigenization of agriculture in Kenya by increasing the dependence of Kenyan agriculture and the Kenyan economy on foreign capital.

The British Government and its allies used indigenization in Kenya as an opportunity to accelerate the capitalist penetration of Kenya. Already, the pre-independence Government which had insisted on the payment of the full market value for the settled European farms had asserted the right to private property. The institution of private property was further reinforced by the Government's refusal to turn the land bought from the Europeans into state farms or to give it freely to Africans and make the settlement loans a public debt. The settlement loans were used to further capitalist penetration by being tied to the land registration programme which the Colonial Government had started. On the direction of the Kenyan Colonial Government, a senior civil servant, R.J.M. Swynnerton, had drawn up a *Plan to Intensify the Development of African Agriculture* in 1953. This document was the basis of a massive programme for consolidating and registering land under individual freehold titles — a necessary condition of capitalist agriculture. As was to be expected, agricultural credit was tied to land registration. By 1960 all of Kikuyuland was already registered and the programme spread to other tribal lands. The settlement loans were used to accelerate this process of land consolidation and registration. By the conditions attached to them, the British Government ensured that the principle of private ownership would prevail in the Europeans' white highlands as well.

Finally, the penetration of Western capitalism into Kenya was greatly facilitated by the debt burden of the settlement schemes. The problem of the debt burden was very serious, as the *Development Plan 1970-74* indicates: 'At the end of 1966 a total of £1.7 million had been billed to settlers, but 55.7% of this amount had not been paid at that date and 23.1% had been in arrears for one year or longer. At the end of 1968 a total of £3.9 million had been billed to settlers but 43.7% of this amount was in arrears and 23.7% had been outstanding for one year or more.' According to the *Economic Survey, 1971*, 44% of the service and repayment charges owed by the new settlers were in arrears. The seriousness of the debt burden necessitated action. The Van Arkadie Mission of 1966 looked into the problem. The report of the Mission showed that the debt burden was quite crippling to the settlers. It pointed out that the new settlers were invariably expected to put about 70% or more of their farm income into debt repayment. Their operation could hardly be viable in such circumstances. The report warned that the 'existing arrangement cannot fail to lead to a financial crisis for the Kenya Government.' As was to be expected, the situation weakened the Kenyan Government and made it even more dependent financially. By 1965 the Kenyan Government was pleading for an incredibly large loan of roughly £35 million.

We can see that if the settlement schemes are to be judged as an attempt to liberate the agricultural sector of the Kenyan economy from Western imperialism, the aim was largely defeated, for one must conclude that the net effect of the scheme has been the deeper entrenchment of the hold of Western capitalist imperialism in Kenya's agriculture. To illustrate, let us look at the Kenyan Government's *Development Estimates for the Year 1971/72*. Of an estimated gross total development expenditure of £6,700,331 for agriculture, £4,399,099 or 59.58% was to come from foreign (Western) sources and only £2,740,232 or 40.42% from local sources. The major thrust of the development budget was crop production for which an estimated gross total expenditure of £2,542,550 was budgeted. It was expected that £1,610,010 or 63.32% would come from Kenya's Western creditors while only £932,540 or 36.68% would come from local sources. Foreign domination of agricultural credit is greater yet. The Agricultural Finance Corporation is the major agricultural credit agency of Kenya. The gross total development budget of the AFC was £2,393,070 of which £1,696,880 or 82.39% was to come from foreign (Western) sources while only £298,810 or 17.61% was expected to be raised locally. Another institution, the Agricultural Development Corporation, expected 79.4% of its development expenditure to come from foreign (Western) sources and only 20.51% from local sources. Finally Western capitalism continues to sponsor the land adjudication and registration programme which, as we have seen, is necessary for the institutionalization of capitalism in Kenya. The 1971/2 development budget projected a gross expenditure of £909,225. As much as 66.54% was to come from foreign sources while only 33.46% was expected from local sources.

It is now time to turn to the question of the relation of the indigenization of agriculture in Kenya to class formation and class interests. The strategy for the indigenization of agriculture which the Government of Kenya has been pursuing is only a further elaboration of the agricultural strategy of the British Colonial Government. The British Government had developed the policy in the wake of the Mau Mau insurrection as a means of pacification and to create an African bourgeoisie with a vested interest in neo-colonialist economic relations. The Government of independent Kenya adopted the strategy with the same effect. That a major aim of the settlement schemes was pacification is rather obvious. The Squatter Settlement Scheme was designed to serve as social relief. It offered some of the destitute and landless the opportunity of staving off starvation by toiling on a small farm. The Government of Kenya hardly concealed its design to use land settlement to procure political stability as cheaply as possible. Here is an example from the *Development Plan 1970-74.*

> 'During the new Plan period, major emphasis will be given to a programme designed to settle about 33,000 squatters, mostly on farms of less than 4 hectares each. The Government appreciates that families settled under this programme will have to be content with smaller incomes than the farmers on the Million Acre Settlement Scheme. However, this programme will have a significant impact on the problems of landlessness and unemployment at relatively low cost, thus leaving a high proportion of public agricultural development funds available for other development programmes.' [9]

Along with the pacification of the destitute, the indigenization of agriculture nurtured the growth of capitalist farming. The major thrust of the settlement scheme (The Million Acre Scheme) went in this direction. As we have seen, the average size of the farms under this scheme was about 12 hectares. Those who had the credit-worthiness to obtain the loans for purchasing the larger farms were people who were already fairly well off, at any rate people who were well connected socially and politically. The Million Acre Settlement Scheme and the whole institution of agricultural credit fostered inequality in Kenya:

> '. . . the great bulk of the development loans — roughly £7.5 million out of 10.5 million — went to the same people who secured land purchase loans. This was even more true of crop finance, nearly all of which went to large farms. Within the roughly £3 million lent to smallholders outside the ex-European areas, it is probable that more than half went to larger farms in the Central Province. There is also a good deal of duplication in the figures; a successful small farmer who repays his first loan satisfactorily is the most acceptable candidate for a second loan.' [10]

The ILO Mission to Kenya has given us a picture of the stratification system that has followed this agricultural strategy. At the top of the pyramid is a group of about 225,000 farmers or about 20% of all smallholders, mainly in the high-potential areas, 'who have rapidly increased their incomes over the past decade. These are for the most part farmers who have benefitted from settlement and irrigation schemes or from land registration.' The core of this group would be the owners of the 1,234 Africanized large-scale mixed farms covering over 500,000 hectares. Mediating between this group and the poorest peasants is another category of about 250,000 smallholders. The members of this group have been able to commercialize their farming with rather limited success. As a general rule they employ seasonal but no permanent labour and their annual farming income is between £60 — £120. At the bottom of the pyramid are the majority of farming families, with about 620,000 smallholdings. [11] These hold very small plots and there is very little they can do to raise productivity which is usually less than £60 a year. 'It is inevitable that at the low level of agricultural production and income, these families must either exist in extreme poverty or must obtain income from sources other than their own farms by seeking work in the rural areas or in the town.' [12] So much for agriculture; let us turn to Kenyanization of commerce and industry.

The policy of indigenization in industry and commerce complemented that of agriculture. One element of this policy was the decision by the Kenyan Government to buy controlling shares in the companies which were particularly important in the economy. For instance the Government acquired 50% interests in the Standard Bank of Kenya and the Barclays Bank, 60% in the Kenya Commercial Bank, 50% in the East African Oil Refineries and 51% in East African Power and Lighting. This line of attack did not accomplish very much as far the liberation of the economy is concerned. The extent of Government participation in these and other bodies indicate that the Government was not seeking to end foreign domination but to forge a partnership with foreign capital. Even if the Kenyan Government had wanted to proceed more aggressively it could not do so because it was too weak. It could participate only by paying its way, but it could not afford to pay its way.

In its policy paper *African Socialism and Its Application to Planning in Kenya*, published in 1965, the Government argued that the money paid out in compensation for nationalization 'would most likely leave the country increasing our foreign exchange problems.' Making a virtue of necessity, the document argued that 'if the nation's limited domestic capital is used to buy existing land, livestock, buildings, machinery and equipment, the nation has no more productive assets than before, only their ownership has changed. What may be lost are the new resources that could have been purchased instead . . . and added output that these developments would create.' The document announced that instead of going for nationalization the Government would concentrate on maximizing African participation in new economic expansion.

The strategy of Kenyanization shifted accordingly. The major instrument of this policy is the Industrial and Commercial Development Corporation, (ICDC), a statutory corporation. The ICDC carries out its function of stimulating and directing commercial and industrial development and furthering African economic participation mainly through a network of subsidiaries. However it retains primary responsibility for providing credit for African businessmen. For this purpose, it operates the ICDC Loan Scheme. The most important subsidiary of ICDC is the Development

Finance Company of Kenya (DFCK) which sponsors investment in new commercially viable projects but not in infrastructure projects. Another subsidiary of ICDC, Kenya National Properties Limited, established in 1968, helps African businessmen to procure suitable business premises by giving them loans, guaranteeing their loans etc. The Kenya National Trading Corporation, another statutory corporation which is also a subsidiary of ICDC, was established in 1965 to promote Kenyanization of wholesale and retail trade and export trade especially in primary products. It promotes Kenyanization partly by its powers of trade licensing and regulation of exports and imports. The National Construction Corporation was established in 1968, and its principal objective was 'to sponsor Kenyan contractors and to encourage others to enter the construction field, by providing loans, guidance etc.'

All this gives the impression of a very strenuous effort at Kenyanization of commerce and industry. But when we look closely we see that it does not amount to much. To begin with, if the Government is to reshape commerce and industry by participating in investment then its contribution to investment has to be a significant portion of the total investment outlay. But this is not the case in Kenya. To illustrate, the Government projected a total investment of £100 million for the plan period 1970-74, but it could only allocate £922,000 for the entire four years. The Government's rationalization is that 'the total amount is less important than the fact that Government is ready to participate on a joint basis with private investors and by so doing, indicate its confidence in particular projects and thereby get them under way more quickly than might otherwise be the case.' [13] The fact of the matter is that the Government has neither the will nor the resources to do more. And because it is unable and unwilling to take more drastic steps, its control of commerce and industrial development is necessarily very limited.

Worse still, ICDC and DFCK, the two major institutions which are supposed to engineer the Kenyanization of industry and commerce, are not even controlled by the Government. The Kenyan Government is in effect a junior partner to Western capital in both of these statutory bodies. It holds only 25% of the shares in DFCK. The other partners, holding the same proportion of shares, are the Commonwealth Development Corporation, the Netherlands Overseas Finance Company and the German Development Corporation. The ICDC consists of exactly the same partnership.

Neither the ICDC nor the DFCK is in a position to exercise much influence over the industrial and commercial development of Kenya. According to the Development Plan 1970-74, the ICDC was scheduled to hold only 16% of the total equity in all ICDC projected investments. This hardly puts the corporation in a position to dictate. The ICDC's record of indigenization inevitably reflects its weaknesses. For instance one of its better known efforts at indigenization was a well advertised programme of

45

buying shares in profitable companies and subsequently selling them to Africans. Colin Leys finds that by 1970 '59% of the shares had been bought by some 1,900 Africans . . . the average shareholding was worth roughly £50 to a total of about £100,000 or 0.02 per cent of the net assets of the thirty-six companies quoted in the Nairobi Stock Exchange in 1970.' [14] In these circumstances, it is hardly surprising that Kenya has not made much progress towards indigenization of her commerce and industry. The ILO Mission which examined Kenya's progress in some detail came to the following conclusion:

'. . . local participation during the period 1960-70 was, on average, 42.8 percent in Japanese investments and 39.9 per cent in Indian investments — but all other sources (including the major investing countries, the United Kingdom and the United States) have less than 25 percent of local participation on the average.

It is therefore reasonable to assume that the "foreign owned" category in table 73 covers virtually all the production by enterprises with foreign equity participation. The table shows that these enterprises accounted for 57 percent of the gross product in 1967. The percentage is probably greater now (possibly over 65 percent), since there have been some large foreign investments in recent years . . . The table shows that foreign enterprises account for a disproportionately large share of profits (73 percent).' [15]

We must now turn to the question of the relation of indigenization policy to the class structure. It is quite obvious that the policies we have examined here will have the effect of promoting partnership between the Kenyan bourgeoisie and Western capitalism. The policies are not aimed at ending the domination of Western capital but only at ensuring that some Kenyans develop a vested interest in it:

'Indeed, the power of the centre over the periphery may well today be greater than before, since there is now a closer correlation of interests between the urban elite, the owners of large farms and the larger, expatriate, companies. Previously, these groups were all headed by non-Africans, mostly Europeans. Though they had a close identity of interest and views, and a way of life and contacts which made it easy to exchange information, there were some respects in which their interests differed.

All these circles are now more closely linked, and coalitions of interests are accordingly closer. Moreover, such coalitions of interests were, before independence at least, conspicuous, and racially vulnerable to nationalist challenges. Kenyanization has significantly reduced this risk. [Not only] within the manufacturing sector but to some extent also in other parts of the economy.' [16]

Finally it should be mentioned that partnership between the Kenyan bourgeoisie and international capitalism was promoted in a manner that consolidated the material base of the Kenyan bourgeoisie. On this score the crucial factor was the decision not to nationalize and socialize foreign assets but to help Kenyan entrepreneurs to become more successful or more competitive. To this end, the ICDC bought shares and sold them to Kenyans; but the Kenyans who could afford to buy into the profitable foreign businesses were the middle class. Colin Leys, commenting on this programme, says 'the share register read like a roll call of the Kikuyu middle classes, who held over 90 percent of the shares sold to individuals.' [17] When the ICDC gave loans, often averaging £3,000, it was only providing opportunities for the rich to get richer for it was only the rich who could procure such loans. The Trade Licensing Acts were used to discriminate against Asian middlemen in order that their African competitors might prosper. The National Properties Limited could not help the Kenyan common man; it was servicing already successful entrepreneurs by acquiring and developing business premises for them. The same is true of the National Trading Corporation.

Nigerian Indigenization: Expansion of a Bourgeoisie

In Nigeria the most notable development in indigenization in recent years is the Nigerian Enterprises Promotion Decree promulgated in March 1972. [18] The decree lists two categories of enterprises. The first category is to be reserved exclusively for Nigerians. Apart from the retail trade and road transport, the category of enterprises reserved exclusively for Nigerians relates to almost entirely marginal sectors of the economy. This list is revealing. Nigerians may monopolize: advertising and public relations agencies, pool betting business and lotteries, assembly of radios, radiograms, record changers, television sets, tape recorders and electric domestic appliances not combined with manufacturing of components, blending and bottling of alcoholic drinks, blocks, bricks and tile manufacturing, bread and cake making, candle manufacture, casinos and gaming centres, cinemas and other places of entertainment, clearing and forwarding agencies, hairdressing, haulage of goods by road, laundry and dry-cleaning, manufacture of jewellery and related articles, newspaper publishing and printing, ordinary garment manufacture not combined with the production of textile materials, municipal bus services and taxis, radio and television broadcasting, retail trade (except by or within the department stores and supermarkets), rice milling, singlet manufacture, tyre retreading.

The second category of enterprises consists of those open to aliens under certain conditions. It embraces far more vital sectors of the economy. The thirty-three enterprises in this list include: wholesale distribution, shipping, construction industries, boat building, furniture making, manufacture of metal containers, manufacture of bicycles, production of sawn timber, plywood, veneers and other wood conversion industries, slaughtering, storage, distribution and processing of meat, poultry farming etc. Foreigners may participate in enterprises in this category under two conditions. First the enterprises must be fairly large ones with capital of over £500,000. Second, there must be 40% Nigerian participation. To ensure the implementation of the decree some other supporting measures were taken. I shall mention only the most important here. Banks were indigenized to the extent of 40% Nigerian ownership and the Government directed that banks follow the guideline of giving 40% of their total loans to Nigerians. By Decree No. 22 of 1973, the Government established The Nigerian Bank of Industry and Commerce mainly to make available credit facilities to Nigerian businessmen. It was stipulated that the bank would not normally grant loans of less than £10,000 to indigenous businessmen seeking to take over foreign businesses in the first category of the indigenization decree. As far as enterprises in the second category are concerned the banks' role consists mainly in underwriting shares offered to the public.

These measures can hardly constitute a serious attack on dependence. First the spheres of economic activity reserved for Nigerians are quite insignificant in terms of their share of GNP. Candle manufacture, hair-dressing, singlet manufacturing, tyre retreading, etc. exert an insignificant influence on the Nigerian economy. In reserving the businesses in Category 1 for Nigerians, the indigenization decrees merely preserved the status quo since these sectors of the economy were almost completely Nigerian already.

Most significantly, the indigenization decree does not bring under Nigerian control the really big enterprises and the multinational corporations which dominate the economy. These include Whiteheads, (a Lonhro subsidiary), Unilever, Tate and Lyle, Turner and Newall, John Holt, (another Lonhro subsidiary), the United African Company, Dunlop, Patterson Zachonis, Barclays Bank, Standard Bank, G.B. Ollivant, United Trading Company, K. Chellarans, Esquire, Bhojsons, Societe Commerciale Orientale d'Afrique etc. The failure to indigenize these enterprises is all the more surprising because they not only dominate the economy, they are also profitable. For instance, according to a report in the *Daily Times*, Monday July 15, 1974, the United African Company made a profit of £22 million.

It would appear that the significance of the indigenization decree lies not so much in its contribution to the liberation of the Nigerian economy as in its contribution to the consolidation of the hold of the ruling class in Nigeria. The decree helps the successful indigenous capitalists to become more successful still, virtually offering them wealth by giving them money to buy into successful business. In the final analysis, the net effect of the decree will be to increase the inequalities in the distribution of wealth. Not only does it increase the wealth of successful indigenous capitalists relative to the masses, it is also increasing the gap between the petty businessmen and the more successful indigenous capitalists. To understand why this is so, one has to consider the manner in which credit is made available to Nigerians to buy into foreign business. The Nigerian Bank of Industry and Commerce will not in normal circumstances grant loans of less than £10,000. That means that it is interested in loaning money to people in business in a big way. The types of applicants who are sufficiently credit-worthy to make successful applications for loans as well as those who can absorb loans of such magnitude will invariably be well established capitalists. In this context, the indigenization decree is clearly an example of the use of state power to promote the class interests of the big Nigerian capitalists at the expense of other bourgeois elements.

Finally, one effect of the indigenization decree is to rationalize the relationship between the Nigerian bourgeoisie and its patron, international capitalism, in such a manner as to decrease the chances of serious conflict between them. The decree limits the chances of conflict by a clearer demarcation of spheres. It reserves a sphere of influence for Nigeria's marginal capitalists, and international capitalism is to refrain from interfering in this sphere. Such restraint is clearly necessary to contain the potentially dangerous economic nationalism of the petty bourgeoisie. The decree integrates the Nigerian bourgeoisie with international capitalism by involving them in business partnerships to a greater degree than ever before. The authors of the decree admit this. [19] Finally the decree underlines the partnership and common interests of the military/bureaucratic faction and the commercial/industrial faction of the Nigerian bourgeoisie. In these ways, the decree is consolidating the ruling class and its power to survive.

This discussion would not be complete without mention of the petroleum industry, which deserves particular attention partly because of its importance for the Nigerian economy and partly because indigenization in this sector of the Nigerian economy appears uncharacteristically bold. Far from being bold, indigenization in the oil industry has been characteristically timid, reflecting the weaknesses of the Nigerian bourgeoisie.

To understand why this is so, one has to appreciate the oil sector's sudden rise to domination of the Nigerian economy. In the fiscal year 1970/71 oil accounted for only 27.4% of the Federal Government's revenue while the share of the revenue from sources other than oil was 72%. By the fiscal year 1974/75 there is a drastic reversal. Oil now accounts for 84.4% while revenue from non-oil sources only amounts to 15.6%. In 1974 the Nigerian Government decreed Government participation of up to 55% in oil companies. Given the fact that the Nigerian economy is now for all practical purposes a petroleum economy, this 55% indigenization is hardly bold; it is rather like a Government deciding to control half of its economy. The extent of indigenization of the oil sector is all the more revealing given the high profits of the sector: to illustrate, a Nigerian newspaper, the *Daily Times*, calculated that the acquisition of 55% of the oil sector cost the Nigerian Government £780 million. [20] But the net return on the Government's investment is expected to be £5,000 million, at least.

Tanzanian Indigenization: State Capitalism

The Tanzanian experience presents a very interesting contrast to Nigeria and Kenya. The major tool of indigenization in Tanzania is the parastatal system. According to a Tanzanian Government source a parastatal is a commercial enterprise 'owned by the government or with majority government participation and run on commercial principles and whose accounts are not directly integrated into the government budgets.'[21] According to the *Presidential Circular on the Nationalization of the Parastatal Organization*, 'The overall structure must be such that increasing public enterprise and public economic initiative can continue to be effectively controlled and coordinated by the Government as the economy expands.' [22] Among the earliest parastatals were the Tanzania Electric Supply Company (TANESCO) and the Tanganyika Development Corporation (TDC) which were founded in 1963. But the parastatal system in Tanzania developed mainly in the wake of the *Arusha Declaration* when Tanzanian leaders opted for socialism and self-reliance. The declaration was followed by a crop of parastatals, and these organizations have proliferated since. Of all the parastatals the largest and most functionally diffuse is the National Development Corporation (NDC) formed from TDC in 1965. The NDC is supposed to be the architect of Tanzania's industrialization. There is also a system of financial parastatals which include the Bank of Tanzania, the Central Bank of Commerce (CBC), the Tanzania Development Finance Co. (TDFC), the Tanzania Investment Bank (TIB) and the Tanzania Rural Development Bank (TRDB). Agriculture also has its system of parastatals which include the National Agricultural and Food Corporation (NAFCO) and the National Agricultural Company (NAC). Retail trade is dominated by the State Trading Corporation (STC) and tourism by the Tanzania Tourist Corporation (TTC). The industrial sector is coming increasingly under the NDC and its subsidiaries. The number of parastatals in Tanzania was 43 in 1966. By 1973 it had risen to 112. As a result of this development the public sector is much stronger in the economy. It accounted for 60% of the monetary fixed capital formation in 1969. [23]

How far has Tanzania succeeded in liberating her economy from foreign domination? Not very much. The old pattern of trade dependence on the capitalist West still persists, although there has been considerable improvement in this respect. But more importantly Tanzania continues to rely heavily on foreign capital, (particularly from the West). To illustrate, 56.1% of the 1971/72 development budget was to come from external sources; for the financial year 1972/73 the proportion of the development budget expected from foreign sources was 62.8%; in 1973/74 it was 54% and the prognostications indicate that for 1974/75 it will be over 55%.[24]

The Tanzanian economy looks much more socialized and nationalized because of the proliferation of the parastatals and their evident influence. It is all too easy to move from the fact that a sector of the economy is controlled by a public corporation to unfounded assumptions based on the connotations of the phrase 'public corporation'. The crucial question is, of course, who controls the parastatals. The answer is by no means simple. Let us start with the assumption that Tanzania holds 100% of all the shares of the parastatals. Even then we do not have a conclusive answer to the question, for the distribution of shares is not necessarily the most important criterion for determining the locus of control. In the case of Tanzania, the fact that the public corporations are highly dependent on foreign funds for their activities is very significant. The extent of the dependence of the parastatals on foreign capital is brutally clear from the table below.

Percentages of Parastatal Expenditure	1967/70	1970/71	1971/72	1972/73	1973/74
Non-Aided Projects	74	68	22	7	13
Aided Projects of which	26	32	78	93	87
(a) Local	13	12	22	20	28
(b)Foreign	13	20	56	73	59
TOTAL	100	100	100	100	100

Adapted from *The Annual Plan for 1972/73* (Dar es Salaam, 1972).

The financial dependence of the parastatals reveals itself as even more serious when we relax the assumption of 100% Tanzanian ownership. Although there are parastatals in which Tanzania owns 100% of the shares, it would appear that the more usual pattern is majority public ownership with foreign participation. If we remember these factors, it is not so puzzling that Tanzania has achieved very limited indigenization despite her elaborate parastatal system. In Tanzania, as everywhere else in Africa, the consequences of the indigenization effort for the liberation of the economy have been far more ambiguous than its effect on the availability of power resources to the ruling class. The enormous expansion of the public sector has given Tanzania's rulers access to more resources and more patronage; it has increased the penetrative capacity of political power.

Tanzania's attempt at indigenization via expansion of the state's economic role and public takeovers of foreign firms shows up the difficulties of even an indigenization strategy that does not rely on the creation of an indigenous bourgeoisie within the private sector. Let us give an idealized account of the difficult decisions that Tanzania had to make.

Assume that at independence or shortly afterwards Tanzania was determined to end her economic dependence, and further that she decided to do this by nationalizing foreign assets. She would immediately have to make difficult choices about the terms of the nationalization, particularly whether or not to pay compensation. Now the option of refusing to pay compensation did not really exist given the heavy dependence of Tanzania on Western capitalism; the West was in such control that it could quite easily have engineered the complete collapse of the Tanzanian economy. And the nationalist leadership which succeeded the colonial regime was hardly in a position to risk this option; its power was still too fragile because of its weak material base, its political grip on the country was still uncertain and was made more so by the confusion of transition. So quite naturally Tanzania, like other African countries, felt it necessary to opt for nationalization with compensation. But that only created a new dilemma. Where would the money be found to pay the requisite compensation ? In the face of this dilemma, some countries such as Kenya backtracked and chose to nationalize less. But others, notably Tanzania, pressed on with nationalization and incurred a heavy debt burden. But if this were paid from the country's meagre reserves, the economy would come under too much pressure; in any case it is doubtful whether any African country has the resources to buy back her economy. If, on the other hand, it was paid with external loans as Kenya tended to do, then dependence was not attacked but merely recycled. As we have seen, in the case of Kenya, the policy of borrowing money to buy back the economy only increased the country's financial dependence.

The solution which appealed to many African countries including Tanzania was to pay for the acquisition of foreign equity over time, largely out of profits. But even this was hardly a way out. To begin with, the country was still in the unhappy position of toiling to pay those who had exploited it in the past. The burden of debt also limited its independence. To understand the extent of this limitation, we have to remember how a country's attitude to her creditors affects the availability of the external funds on which Africa so heavily depends. But these are not even the worst disadvantages of the solution under review. The choice of this option was generally made on the assumption that the nationalized enterprises would continue to be profitable, so the debt could be paid. The principle of profitability invariably leads to management agreements with the previous foreign owners of the nationalized assets. These agreements defeat the original purpose of nationalization by giving foreign managers extensive control of production planning, machinery acquisition, marketing information etc. It is easy to see that the principle of profitability would be particularly unfortunate in a case like Tanzania's which is trying to combine indigenization with socialism. To the extent that the criterion of profitability asserts itself, a socialist system will not evolve. At best what will evolve will be state capitalism — a system of capitalist relations of production in which the government and public corporations play the role of the capitalist exploiter. This brief discussion shows why economic dependence on the West and capitalism will tend to perpetuate themselves even where genuine desire to remove them exists. The economic conditions that make indigenization of African economies so desirable also render it extremely difficult to achieve. In short, there is no economic solution to the problem of indigenization. The problem — and the solution — are ultimately political.

CONCLUSIONS

These case studies show that the pursuit of indigenization of African economies has been subordinated to the consolidation of the power of the ruling class in each case and has indeed been used as a means of such consolidation. They also show that the thrust of indigenization is not so much the elimination of neo-colonial dependence as the establishment of a new accommodation with it.

It is all the more interesting that very little indigenization has been achieved when one considers that the African bourgeoisie has much to gain from indigenization. There are considerable contradictions between the interests of this bourgeoisie and the metropolitan bourgeoisie, contradictions which have become clearer in the course of the global class struggle. The global class struggle has, by underlining these contradictions, also underlined the need for both the African bourgeoisie and the metropolitan bourgeoisie to be more independent of each other.

Why has so little been done about indigenization despite all this ? It is because the African bourgeoisie is an integral part of the structure of dependence. Without implying that capitalism did not exist in Africa before colonialism, one might say that the particular brand of capitalism which exists in Africa today was created by imperialism. It was created as a dependency capitalism, incorporating structural characteristics which reinforce dependence even as this capitalism develops. The African bourgeoisie is also a creation of imperialism; it is the self-reproduction of the metropolitan bourgeoisie, in caricature as it were. It is a historically determinate form of the extension of the metropolitan bourgeoisie for the purposes of accumulation on a world scale. The African bourgeoisie shares to a considerable extent the consciousness, the tastes and life-style of the metropolitan bourgeoisie; this is what the popular phrase 'colonial mentality' really refers to. Most importantly, the common interest of both the African and the metropolitan bourgeoisies is to maintain the existing exploitative relations of production in Africa. Imperialism exploits Africa through these exploitative relations. The African bourgeoisie survives and exploits the African masses in so far as these exploitative relations of production are maintained. In short, the African bourgeoisie is an integral part of the structure of dependence. It is part of the problem, in a sense the very core of the problem of indigenization which it is supposed to solve. Even if one takes the popular view that indigenization is a matter of fighting imperialism, this conclusion still holds. For, in the African context at least, the fight against imperialism must also be a fight against capitalism. To the extent that one is fighting capitalism in Africa, one is of course fighting the African bourgeoisie. In order to avoid misunderstanding, I should add that the assumption here is not that if there is no capitalism in Africa there is no problem of dependence, or of indigenization. The point being made here is that as far as the African situation is concerned, the abolition of capitalist relations of production is a necessary preliminary to the realization of indigenization.

I will dwell briefly on the view of indigenization as a problem of fighting imperialism because it clarifies certain points. Assume that the African bourgeoisie was not in fact part of the structure of dependence as suggested and that it was determined to do battle against imperialism. What would such a battle mean in terms of public policy ? It would mean Africa's wholesale disengagement from exploitative relations with international capital. It would entail having to do without most of the apparatus of international aid, imported technology and imported consumer goods. The African country which decided to nationalize without compensation and to end exploitative ties with international capital would invite severe reprisals including a determined attempt to cause its economic and political disintegration. The African country which decided to buy back its economy would in all probability plunge into even more extreme poverty in the short run. Drastic reduction or total elimination of dependence on foreign aid, technical assistance, management agreements, etc. would, most likely, cause a very sharp drop in living standards. How could a society withstand the strains and stresses of indigenization ? What kind of society could carry out indigenization without disintegrating ? It would have to be a society which possessed ideological clarity down to the grassroots. It would have to be a society in which antagonistic contradictions did not exist between the leaders and the masses. With few exceptions, the societies of contemporary Africa are far from meeting these conditions. They are riddled with class divisions and antagonistic contradictions. The general trend in contemporary Africa is the consolidation of the dictatorship of the bourgeoisie, a process that has revealed and sharpened the contradictions between the bourgeoisie and the masses in Africa. If indigenization is pursued under these conditions it will in all probability lead to political and economic collapse. Moreover, in the absence of popular goodwill to fall back on, the hardships of indigenization can only have the effect of enormously increasing revolutionary pressures from below while cutting off the all important support of the metropolitan bourgeoisie.

We can readily understand why the African bourgeoisie has done so little to realize indigenization. Quite understandably, it refused to commit suicide. And yet by shying away from indigenization, the African bourgeoisie may well be choosing another form of suicide. This is so because by maintaining neo-colonial dependence, which lies behind Africa's under-development, the African bourgeoisie deepens and radicalizes the contra-dictions in existing relations of production and hence promotes its own revolutionary liquidation.

3

THE CLASS STRUGGLE

In this chapter I want to outline the class structure of contemporary Africa and to show how the dynamics of class affect the prospects of overcoming underdevelopment. I hope that this exercise will throw further light on the necessity and possibility of socialist revolution in Africa. In particular I hope to show how the African bourgeoisie constitutes an obstacle to development, even capitalist development, and how the survival of this class is threatened by the perpetuation of underdevelopment.

So far, I have taken for granted the division of Africa into exploiting and exploited classes. This is in fact a crucial and difficult assumption which cannot be taken for granted, especially in the examination of the domestic situation in Africa. I will accordingly address myself to this assumption and will begin by looking more closely at the concept of class.

THE LABOUR PROCESS AND THE CONCEPT OF CLASS

It might be said that man is, more than anything else, a 'labourer'. He must labour to maintain and reproduce himself and the conditions associated with his existence. This assertion is true of man in all stages of social evolution. It is tempting to assume that at a very primitive stage one may legitimately think of man not as a labourer but as a consumer, simply feeding off the prodigality of nature. But the temptation ought to be resisted. To being with, even plucking ripe fruit or taking fish from the river entails labour; a minimal degree of labour, to be sure, but labour all the same. In any case, as Marx points out, 'conditions in which man need merely reach for what is already available . . . are very transitory, and can nowhere be regarded as normal, not even as normal in the most primitive state.'

Labouring, or better still the labour process, is primarily, or at any rate originally, an interaction between man and nature, appropriating the fruits of nature directly for consumption or converting raw materials into tools for use in bending nature to his needs. As he interacts with nature in this way, man transforms nature, transforms himself and the conditions of his existence; this interaction is in effect the dynamic of social evolution, including the evolution of social classes.

To understand the relation of this interaction to the formation of social classes, we need to look at the labour process more closely. Following Marx, I decompose the labour process into three elements. The first element is labour itself; i.e. the totality of intellectual and physical attributes of man which enables him to work; we may for the sake of simplicity think of this element as labour power. The second element, objects of labour, consists of those objects at which man directs his labour or 'mixes his labour' with: for instance the land which man cultivates for food and the ocean from which he catches fish or obtains water. The third element is the instruments of labour, that is to say the tools with which man labours. Not surprisingly, Marx gives this element a special importance among the elements of the labour process. Even in the most primitive of societies, man is rarely able to appropriate nature without mediation by instruments of labour. Instruments of labour are the link between labour power and the objects of labour. On the one hand, they make it possible for labour power to be realized, to be expressed as a concrete process. On the other hand, they are the means by which nature is transformed to satisfy human needs. Without the instruments of labour, neither labour power nor nature can be harnessed to satisfy man's needs, and hence the conditions for man's reproduction effectively disappear.

The concept of class is primarily, at any rate initially, a description of man's relationship to nature. Or better yet, it is a classification of men in terms of their ability to harness nature for the reproduction of the conditions of their existence. In its simplest and most fundamental sense, the classification is a dichotomy between those whose relationship to nature is such that they are unable to harness nature for the purposes of producing and reproducing themselves and those who are able to do so. Put another way, there are those who possess the vital element in the labour process, the instruments of labour, and those who do not. Those who belong to the first category are the exploiting class and those who belong to the second category are the exploited class. The former are able to exploit because, possessing the instruments of production or the objective conditions of labour, they have a stranglehold on those who do not. More specifically the exploitation usually takes the form of the appropriation of surplus value from those who do not possess the instruments of labour. They are forced to give up the use-value of their labour power in return for part of its exchange value. Sheer survival compels them to this transaction for without access to the objects of labour they cannot live. The monopolizers of the instruments of labour have a different motivation: what they pay for labour power in wages is less than the value of the output of that labour; in other words the transaction enables them to live off the sweat of others.

It is clear from this brief account that a class can exist only in relation to another social class, as part of a system of classes. It is equally clear that classes are mutually exclusive, that the relationship between them is essentially one of opposition and contradiction. And yet there is a sense in which classes are complementary for they are elements of the social division of labour. What I am putting forward here is, for all practical purposes, an economic conception of class. Like Rodolfo Stavenhagen, I am of the opinion that 'only if we take the relation to the means of production as the fundamental criterion for the determination of social class is it possible to link these classes to the social structure and to arrive at a structural analysis of society and at sociological and historical explanation.'

I have offered a very elementary account of the concept of class which makes it look uncomplicated. But once we go beyond abstraction and try to apply the concept concretely, all sorts of problems begin to appear. For instance, it is quite difficult to classify members of a historical society according to the criterion of possessing means of production or having access to objective conditions of labour. It would seem that even in the developed industrial societies which are generally agreed to be class societies, there are not many people who cannot be said to possess means of production of some sort. It may be said with some justification that if almost everyone appears to possess means of production, it must be because one is admitting a trivial conception of means of production or of the objective conditions of labour. But this does not help very much because the distinction between a trivial and non-trivial conception of means of production is itself highly problematic.

To some extent, Marx's work helps us to get around this problem; he tries to identify the relevant means of production for a given historical setting. This is contained in the idea that the different epochs have their specific modes of production. Thus in the age of feudalism we can presumably resolve the question of the membership of the two major classes by asking who owns the land; in the capitalist epoch the question will be who owns the capital.

While this is very useful, it is only a very crude solution to the problem. When we characterize an epoch by a mode of production, we are really identifying a dominant or primary or most widely prevalent means of production. That does not really resolve the original problems of what is admissible as a means of production and who is admissible as the exploiting class or the exploited class. Or perhaps it might be more accurate to say that it resolves the problem only partially by giving us one criterion, albeit the major one, for deciding what the means of production are, and for deciding who has access to the objective conditions of labour.

This problem is tied up with another intricate problem; are class relations to be seen in dichotomous terms, and does the analytic utility of the concept of class depend on seeing it in this way ? The account of the concept of class given here uses a simple dichotomous distinction between those who own means of production and those who do not. Marx did not leave the matter at that. He allowed for the possibility of there being more than two classes in the same society at the same time. He was inclined to see three major classes in the society of his time, wage labourers, capitalists and landlords.

Nevertheless, the core ideas of Marx's concept of class imply the notion of the existence of only two classes in a given society at any one time. These core ideas which we find in Volume I of *Capital* are that class refers to relation to the means of production and that class membership is decided in terms of ownership or non-ownership of the means of production. These ideas and the implication of there being only two classes are clear in Engels' famous note in the 1888 English edition of the *Communist Manifesto:*

> 'By the bourgeoisie is meant the class of modern capitalists, owners of the means of social production and employers of wage labour. By proletariat, the class of modern wage labourers who, having no means of production of their own, are reduced to selling their labour power in order to live.'

The same theme appears in the very first section of the *Communist Manifesto:*

> 'The history of all hitherto existing society is the history of class struggles. Freeman and slave, patrician and plebeian, lord and serf, guild master and journeyman, in a word, oppressor and oppressed, stood in constant opposition to each other.'

One should also bear in mind Lenin's famous definition of classes:

> 'Classes are large groups of people which differ from each other by the place they occupy in a historically determined system of social pro-duction, by their relation . . . to the means of production . . . Classes are groups of people, one of which can appropriate the labour of another owing to the different places they occupy in a definite system of social economy.'

I think it a serious theoretical inconsistency to move from the core ideas of the Marxian concept of class to posit that more than two classes can exist in one society at one time — and it is an inconsistency which will have the practical effect of drastically diminishing the analytic value of the concept of class. Consider the idea of a society with three classes: workers, landlords, and capitalists. Applying the two elements which define class relations, namely the mode of production and the distribution of owner-ship of the means of production within this mode, we may say that in the pair workers and capitalists we have a class system. The class, landlords, is totally incongruent with the other two classes: it does not belong with them to a system of classes because it refers to a different mode of pro-duction. If we consider landlords *sui generis*, we only pass into absurdity, for a class cannot exist alone. A society with only one class is a classless society, a society to which the concept of class no longer applies.

All this is rather obvious. The issue is not really whether we can have a society of three classes but whether we can have a society of more than two classes. I will modify my example and consider a society of four classes, namely workers, capitalists, landlords and peasants. This classification is not vulnerable to the types of criticism levelled against the previous example of a three class society. Does that mean that there is no problem of having a society with more than two classes ? The answer must be no. And yet the idea of a society of four or more classes seems perfectly defensible and not at all extraordinary especially in 'transitional' societies such as the societies of Africa, where different modes of production are juxtaposed. For instance, an African society with vestiges of capitalism and feudalism might be said to have four classes, peasants, workers, landlords and capitalists. However much this may appeal to commonsense, it is never-theless invalid. Whatever else a class is, it is a relation (in production) — in the Marxian tradition at any rate. Now if we have four classes (or any number of classes for that matter) the (production) relation of all these classes must be the same, otherwise we are using different definitions of class simultaneously. But what relation (in production) is symmetrical and identical for every relational permutation of all four classes in question — peasant/capitalist, peasant/worker, worker/landlord, landlord/ capitalist etc.?

While the notion of a society with more than two classes rests on a con-fusion, it was in fact born of an attempt to deal with legitimate concerns. If classes are conceived in terms of antagonistic relations between owners and non-owners of the means of production, it is all too easy to ignore the crucial implications for class analysis of the juxtaposition of different modes of production in one economy. For example, thinking only in terms of those who own means of production and those who do not could easily obscure the importance of the division within each of these groups, divisions corresponding to the different modes of production. Also it is quite easy to forget that one is dealing with relations of production which are not so coherent and in which the process of 'exploitation' (for instance of peasants by capitalists) is mediated by many factors and becomes rather complex. These surely are legitimate concerns. However, they are poorly served by talking of three, four or more classes existing all at once in the same society. Doing so does not help us in the least to grapple with the problems of the exploitative relation between, say, peasant and capitalist; at best it encour-ages us to think of pairs of classes whose relationship is obscure. Moreover, while it draws attention to important contradictions, (i.e. those associated with the co-existence of different modes of production), it invites mis-construction of the status of the contradictions between owners and non-owners of means of production.

I have been dealing with the basics of the concept of class. Unfortunately it is not possible to get a full appreciation of the concept of class and its problems and possibilities unless one goes beyond these basics. Here again I will use Marx as my point of departure. Marx suggests that even though the relations of production are the foundation of classes, classes become socially significant groups only when their members become conscious of their interests as a class and the opposition of these interests to the interests of the other class; in short, only when class contradictions become politicized. For instance, in *The Eighteenth Brumaire of Louis Bonaparte*, Marx says of classes that insofar as 'the identity of their interests begets no community no national bond and no political organization among them, they do not form a class.' In saying this, Marx is not superseding or nullifying what we have described as the core ideas of class, he is really offering a further elaboration of the concept based on these core ideas. The politicization of the basic contradiction in production relations is a development which eventually follows once the contradiction exists. Once more, the contradiction is basic in the sense that, among other things, it determines people's role in production, the distribution of the product and eventually the capacity to enjoy freedom, pursue culture, acquire status, political power etc. As the forces of production develop and the consequences of the basic contradiction become evident especially in distribution and consumption, the consciousness of the exploited class begins to grow too. At first, it expresses itself in a rather 'confused' and sporadic manner, for instance in the smashing of machines at the factory. These forms of expression radicalize the contradictions and help to make the consciousness more articulate and expressly political.   What Marx is saying in the passage quoted above is that it is in the eventual politicization of class interests, that is in the eventual emergence of the political class struggle, that the significance of the basic contradiction in the relations of production fully reveals itself as the dynamic of history.

While these points give depth to the concept of class, they also compound the empirical problem of deciding where classes exist and where class analysis may be usefully applied. At what point do we decide that politicization of the basic contradiction in production relations has occurred ? This turns out to be a difficult question once we refrain from limiting ourselves to the most manifest and familiar kinds of politicization and remember that politicization can be masked and 'distorted' in all kinds of ways. For instance, class conflict may be disguised as ethnic or religious conflict, and political conflicts — even very serious ones — may not have a class base.

Passages such as the one quoted from *The Eighteenth Brumaire of Louis Bonaparte* could easily be used to deny the existence of classes and the applicability of class analysis to most contemporary Third World countries. That would be incorrect. The passage in question is telling us what class is in its full maturity and the condition in which the basic contradiction in the relations of production fully reveals its social significance. To deny the existence of classes on the basis of this passage would be to confuse the proposition that something does not exist with the proposition that it does not yet exist in its full maturity. Like most things, classes do not maintain the state in which they came into existence throughout their history. They undergo change. And the passage under discussion is not defining class as such but describing class as it is during a crucial stage in its

61

metamorphosis. More specifically it is describing class as it is *for itself* as opposed to class as it is *in itself*.

The question of the applicability of class analysis to Third World countries is thus still unresolved. Does one postpone the application of class analysis to a society until it has developed to the point when class contradictions are politicized, when the social significance of class contradiction can be fully revealed ? Such postponement would surely be a serious mistake. If we can make a case for the existence of a basic (that is class) contradiction in relations of production, we make a case for class analysis also. For even before the contradiction matures, becomes politicized and radicalized, it is pregnant with the future and remains decisive for the division of labour, production, distribution of the product, consumption etc. The effect of a class situation on society does not depend simply on the consciousness by members of that society of the class situation. However, class analysis of a society with an immature class situation is full of hazards, especially for crude determinists. In what follows, account will be taken of the hazards but no separate theoretical treatment of them will be attempted here.

THE CLASS STRUCTURE OF AFRICA

Are there classes in Africa ? What is the class structure of contemporary Africa ? Objective class relations exist in Africa. There are those who effectively control the means of production, and those who effectively possess no means of production. However, each of these classes is complex and considerably heterogenous.

Who are the members of these classes ? First there is the exploiting class, which consists of the following categories of people.

(a) *Exploiters by class situation.* Everyone who is a capitalist proper. That is everyone who owns capital and employs wage labour in industry, commerce or agriculture.

(b) *Exploiters by class position.* Those who, while not legally owning means of production, play a major role in administering or actualizing exploitation, and maintaining its conditions. They are usually salaried people who hold important positions in the administrative, cultural and coercive apparatus of the state. Members of this category are the officer corps of the armed forces and the police, high ranking civil servants and employees of parastatal bodies, and university teachers. There are several contradictions within this category. Perhaps the most interesting, analytically and politically, is that between those associated with the cultural apparatus of the state, particularly university teachers, and those associated with the coercive apparatus of the state, particularly the officer corps of the armed forces.

Turning to the exploited class, the picture is somewhat simpler. The members of this class are the peasants and the urban proletariat. Like the exploiter class, this exploited class is also heterogenous although it is much less riddled with contradictions. The heterogeneity of this class arises mainly from two factors. One is the coexistence of capitalist and pre-capitalist modes of production. In this connection the major division is that between peasants and workers. However this contradiction is blunted somewhat by what I may call, for lack of a better term, the ruralization of African cities. African primordial solidaristic ties have shown a remarkable resiliency in the face of the onslaught of capitalism. Many workers remain peasants at heart, keep a foot in the village and regard the village as home. One of the striking features of urbanization in Africa is the re-creation of the village community in the city as a basis for recreational activities and for economic and social security. The other source of the incoherence of the exploited class lies in regionalism and the states of consciousness which go with it, especially tribalism.

I have usually referred to the exploited class in Africa as the African proletariat. A note on this usage is necessary; strictly speaking it is inaccurate. Only a small minority of the African masses are workers, the overwhelming majority are peasants; I am using proletariat to include not only workers but peasants. Why not simply describe the exploited class in Africa as the peasantry ? I prefer the term proletariat for the following reasons. First, I wish to emphasize that this exploited class is the subordinate class in essentially capitalist economies. Second, calling the class a peasantry leads to misleading expectations of their mode of exploitation. The manner of exploitation of peasants in an economy dominated by capitalists is somewhat different from their manner of exploitation in an economy dominated by landlords. Finally, the use of the term peasantry leads to misleading expectations about the status and character of the class struggle and the prospects of socialist revolution in Africa. There is a tendency to tie the prospects of achieving socialism too rigidly to the development of productive forces and to assume that peasants are not a revolutionary force. I consider this to be a most unfortunate tendency especially when applied to the African situation, but I will hold off discussion of these issues for later.

So far I have treated the class structure of African countries in a highly undifferentiated manner as if all African countries have exactly the same type of class structure. There are in fact many differences between the class structures of African countries. But I will not try to deal with all these differences and their significance. I will limit myself to what I consider to be the most important difference, which also constitutes the basis of the most useful and most fundamental typology of African political systems.

This difference does not appear on the level of the exploited class, those I have called the African proletariat. It lies in the extent of the development of the African bourgeoisie. We may divide African countries into two groups, with reference to this development. The first group consists of those countries in which colonial policies and/or the development of the forces of production made possible the existence of a small African bourgeoisie, that is an indigenous class of capitalists. I should emphasize that when I talk of an African bourgeoisie or an indigenous capitalist, I do not mean to suggest anything about the independence of this class, that is the lack of comprador characteristics. I am simply describing a group of people who can mobilize and deploy capital, and engage in accumulation, confronting their victims as capital against labour. Among the African countries which belong to this type are Egypt, Nigeria, Ghana, Ivory Coast, Kenya, Morocco and Senegal. The second group of African countries are those in which colonial policies and/or the development of the forces of production has not permitted the emergence of even an embryonic bourgeoisie. There is still class differentiation in these countries, but it is more accurate to describe the dominant class as a petty bourgeoisie rather than a bourgeoisie. It is, to use Cabral's phrase, a 'service class', which is not involved directly in production by mobilizing, deploying and manipulating capital for accumulation. The members of this service class include intellectuals, bureaucrats, and the managers of the coercive machinery of the state. However, the petty bourgeoisie also includes some social groups which are not strictly servicing capitalist accumulation, groups such as petty traders, middle echelon professionals, teachers etc. Countries which fall into this category include Angola, Benin, Botswana, Burundi, Chad, Congo, Ethiopia, Guinea, Mali, Niger, Rwanda, Somalia, Sudan, Mozambique, Tanzania, Upper Volta and Togo.

I mentioned that colonial policies and the level of the development of productive forces largely account for the differences in class structure under review here. I should add that these two variables are also partially dependent on another factor, namely the natural resource endowments of the country. Countries with more substantial resource endowments tended to be the ones in which colonial policy led to a greater development of productive forces and the process of class formation. Here again there are intervening variables. To mention just one, the type of resource endowment dictated the extent of investment in infrastructures and auxiliary services. This helps to explain why Zaire and Angola do not have an indigenous bourgeoisie despite their substantial resource endowments. However, it would seem that this factor was a rather less important determinant of the class structure of these countries than the expectation on the part of the colonizing power that their colonization would be permanent — an expectation which hindered the creation of an indigenous bourgeoisie. It is difficult to be sure of the relative importance of these factors.

On balance, it would appear that the difference in class structure of the two groups of countries has not only persisted but also become accentuated in the 'post colonial era'. The 'departing' colonizing powers have tried to sustain the small momentum in the development of the productive forces in the few countries where such momentum already existed. It is being sustained to aid the process of class formation and the emergence of a comprador bourgeoisie, and by the natural course of international capital seeking safer and bigger markets and high returns. Thus Nigeria, Algeria, Egypt,

Ivory Coast, Kenya, and Senegal attract more European investment than Ethiopia, Angola, Guinea, Somalia, Mali and Tanzania.

Further refinement of this classification is necessary. There is a very important difference among the countries that are under a petty bourgeoisie as opposed to those under a bourgeoisie. The former countries fall into two categories. The first comprises those countries in which the petty bourgeoisie is striving to turn itself into a bourgeoisie. The second is a residual category of those countries in which the petty bourgeoisie is not trying to transform itself into an indigenous capitalist class. Admittedly this is an unusually difficult distinction. For one thing, every ruling class in Africa has a weak material base and is engaged in consolidating it. The line between consolidating the material base of class rule and exploiting subordinate classes in order to further the development of a capitalist class is often very thin. All the more so because state power is the available instrument for promoting both ends in the particular circumstances of the African experience. Also the ruling class cannot consolidate its material base without appearing to be carrying on capitalist accumulation any more than it can use state power to further capitalist accumulation without masking some capitalist and exploitative tendencies. Nevertheless the indications are that in the vast majority of African countries under the rule of a petty bourgeoisie, the petty bourgeoisie is not both trying to consolidate its material base as well as transform itself into a bourgeoisie. The exceptions are the few countries in which the petty bourgeoisie has shown signs of rather serious commitment to socialism such as Guinea Bissau, Angola and Mozambique. Problematic as these distinctions are, they have to be made. Their importance for understanding what is happening and what is likely to happen in Africa is considerable.

THE AFRICAN BOURGEOISIE AS AN OBSTACLE TO PROGRESS

I will now turn to the major task of this chapter which is to show how underdevelopment is related to the class structure of Africa and how the African bourgeoisie constitutes *the* obstacle to progress.

The hub of the relation of underdevelopment to the class structure is the fact that, with few exceptions, the ruling classes in Africa are an integral part of the structure of imperialism and of the syndrome of imperialist exploitation. I have already spelled out how the relation of the ruling classes to imperialism prevents the solution of the problem of indigenization. Up to a point, I have already dealt with the relation of underdevelopment to class structure insofar as underdevelopment is a function of exploitative links between African economies and imperialism, indigenization being the removal of these exploitative links. But this is only one aspect of a complex phenomenon.

AFRICAN RULING CLASSES AND THE WESTERN IDEOLOGY OF DEVELOPMENT

Another aspect of the relationship of underdevelopment to the class structure of contemporary Africa is the developmental ideology of the ruling classes of Africa. They pursue the task of economic development in the context of an ideological orientation which essentially accepts the developmental precepts of the metropolitan bourgeoisie. Surprisingly enough, even the radical (socialism-oriented) African leaders are hardly an exception in this respect. In an earlier discussion, I pointed out that the bourgeois countries use the ideology of development in the global class struggle and that this ideology has come to be hegemonic. The attitudes of Africa's rulers to the ideology of development is interesting for it reflects the identities and differences of their objective interests with those of the metropolitan bourgeoisie. African leaders are critical of the ideology of development and sometimes appear to reject it. They talk constantly of the uniqueness of the African experience and of following a unique path to development. An example of this attitude is to be found in Kenya's famous ideological blueprint, *Sessional Paper No. 10 of 1965: African Socialism and Its Applications to Planning in Kenya:*

> 'In the phrase "African Socialism", the word "Africa" is not introduced to describe a continent to which a foreign ideology is to be transplanted. It is meant to convey the African roots of a system that is itself African in its characteristics. "African Socialism" is a term describing an African political and economic system that is positively African, not being imported from any country or being a blueprint of any foreign ideology but capable of incorporating useful and compatible techniques from whatever source.'

The same type of attitude pervades Nyerere's *Freedom and Unity*. The following passage is typical of the thrust of that work:

> 'Ujamaa, then, or familyhood, describes our socialism. It is opposed to capitalism, which seeks to build a happy society on the basis of the exploitation of man by man; and it is equally opposed to doctrinaire socialism which seeks to build its happy society on a philosophy of inevitable conflict between man and man.'

African leaders have also been quite critical of the bourgeois countries' attitude to development, particularly for not being humanistic and for emphasizing economic growth rather than development. Tanzania's *Mwongozo*, or *TANU Guidelines*, is an excellent example of this type of criticism.

These critical attitudes express the contradiction between the African ruling classes and the metropolitan bourgeoisie on one level as well as those between the bourgeois countries and the proletarian countries. The contents of these criticisms invariably reflect a type of consciousness which is associated with colonial status. For instance, take the strident assertion of uniqueness and autonomy; that one's autonomy and uniqueness have to be asserted implies a certain insecurity about them, or at any rate the necessity of rehabilitating them, and this in turn implies their violation.

But it is just as necessary for Africa's rulers to accept the ideology of development, albeit with some modification, as it is for them to be critical of it, for the ideology of development serves their interests as a ruling class. Just how it does so will become clear shortly. Meanwhile, it is necessary to specify that what the African leaders find so congenial about the ideology of development is the very core of this ideology, namely its notion of what the obstacles to development are and how they might be overcome. The ideology of development sees the problem of achieving development as one of overcoming a series of very specific technical obstacles such as low level of savings, limited achievement motivation, low propensity to invest, low productivity, inadequate technology, low wages, regional disparities, inadequate manpower. When the problem of development is conceptualized in this manner, it is quite clear what has to be done to further development; mobilize more capital, invest more, stimulate achievement motivation, etc.

Does the ideology of development serve the objective interests of Africa's rulers ? In what way ? These questions are fairly easy to answer for the vast majority of the ruling classes of Africa, those we have classified as bourgois or petty bourgeois with aspirations of becoming bourgeois. The ideology of development, particularly its analysis of the problem and process of development, helps to conceal class contradictions. The clear implication of this particular approach to development is that the class structure of a country is irrelevant to its prospects for development and if the class structure and class struggle are irrelevant to the prospects for development, then there is no need to do anything about existing relations of production. The ideology of development offers a status quo oriented approach to development. This is precisely one of the major reasons why Western imperialism, which wants to insulate Africa against socialism, is promoting it so zealously.

Second, the ideology of development helps to legitimize dependence, especially economic dependence. The ideology of development conceptualizes development essentially as a process of becoming more like the bourgeois countries; but a proletarian country becomes more like the bourgeois countries insofar as it can acquire some of the specific goods and specific skills which they monopolize. Once the proletarian country accepts this general approach to development, it comes to regard economic dependence as inevitable and even desirable. On this view, dependence ceases to be an unpleasant necessity and a betrayal of the mandate of a leadership which came to power on the wave of a movement to liberate people from colonialism. It is the stigma of this betrayal that African leaders want to avoid and the ideology of development serves them handsomely.

Third, the ideology of development excuses the painfully slow pace of economic development in Africa. As we have seen, it breaks down the process of development into the solution of very specific, largely technical problems. But it is part of the conservative thrust of this ideology that the problems are ones that are solved only in the very long run by slow incremental change. For instance, suppose Tanzania thinks in terms of acquiring the material characteristics of the United States such as sophisticated technology, a complex network of superhighways, etc. How can it possibly acquire, (even assuming the best intentions on the part of its 'developed' patrons), the capital to transform its present condition into anything remotely resembling that of the United States ? In effect the proletarian country which commits itself to the approach to development in question necessarily commits itself to 'slow and sober' progress. If development is accepted as something which comes by very slow progress over an extremely long time, then patience is necessary and what may seem like stagnation or intolerably slow progress passes as the normal course of things. This leaves little room for legitimately criticising the performance of those who lead the drive for development.

Now that we have seen the advantages of this particular approach to development to African leaders, it does not seem so paradoxical that even the few African leaders who have opted for socialism are not entirely immune to the influence of the ideology of development. They too benefit in the above ways although the benefits are marginally less crucial for them than for the other ruling classes of Africa.

It remains to show how the acceptance of the ideology of development by African leaders helps to perpetuate Africa's underdevelopment. The preceding discussion has already given us indications of the relation between the acceptance of this approach to development and the perpetuation of underdevelopment. So I will merely summarize and bring the important points together. To begin with, by misconceiving and distorting the problem of development, the ideology inhibits its solution. For instance the reduction of development to the solution of specific problems does not help at all, because immersion in these technical problems can only bring stagnation. Given Africa's resources these problems are intractable, and even if they were solved they would not really bring development in any sophisticated sense of the term. While energy is diverted to these technical problems, more crucial bottlenecks which prevent immediate and sizeable progress are neglected. To mention just one neglected bottleneck, there can be no development when those who are to bring development are themselves part of the structure of imperialism. Nor can there be development as long as class contradictions persist and grow. The ideology of development inhibits the development of Africa by effectively masking the link between development and revolution. The experiences of China, the Soviet Union and much of Eastern Europe underline this link. So do the experiences of Western Europe where the achievement of rapid economic growth followed in the wake of the *revolutionary* liquidation of feudalism. In Africa as elsewhere the greatest obstacles to development are social and institutional ones such as class structure, and the vested interests tied up with these obstacles are such that they cannot be removed by anything short of a revolutionary upheaval. Any approach which makes the achievement of development in Africa compatible with the maintenance of the present exploitative relations of production and with the links to imperialism can only hinder Africa.

To sum up, the influence of the ideology of development on the pursuit of development in Africa must be considered as a hindrance to the overcoming of underdevelopment in Africa. This influence prevails mainly because of the objective class situation and class interests of the ruling classes of Africa. I will now turn to the examination of another link between underdevelopment and the class structure of contemporary Africa.

UNDERDEVELOPMENT AND THE UNIQUENESS OF CAPITALISM IN AFRICA

The link I want to examine now has to do with the peculiar characteristics of capitalism in Africa. These peculiarities go back to the colonial legacy. Colonial capitalism was a far cry from the orthodox classical capitalism of Adam Smith's *Wealth of Nations.* For classical capitalism the principle of laisser-faire was sacred. Classical capitalism rejected the authoritative allocation of rewards for work and of price levels; it only accepted the authoritative enforcement of contracts 'freely' entered into in the process of commodity exchange. For classical capitalism, the principle of laisser-faire was important because competition was important. The doctrine of classical capitalism saw competition as the foundation of the efficiency of the capitalist system, and of its dynamism in developing the forces of production; indeed it held that self-interested competition was the means by which the public interest is served. The claim for laisser-faire and competition was of course exaggerated, for competition also leads to waste, misallocation, anarchy in production and monopoly. Nevertheless, competition was a critical element in the dynamism of capitalism. And there is no denying the fact that, in Western Europe, capitalism was a progressive force which has had a most revolutionary effect in transforming and expanding the forces of production.

The same cannot be said of colonial capitalism. An occupying power ruling by force could not institutionalize the principle of laisser-faire. Competition might distribute the wealth more than was desirable; it could lead to some concentration of wealth in the hands of some of the indigenous people and this could endanger the regime, as economic power is easily transformed into political power. If the indigenous people were allowed to compete and become successful, this would undermine the colonial doctrine which represented them as less than human in order to justify their inhuman treatment. The policy compatible with this doctrine was one which denied them access to economic advancement and kept them thoroughly wretched. So the colonial peoples largely lost the advantages of capitalism insofar as these were associated with competition. But this is putting it so mildly as to run the risk of misrepresentation. In the final analysis the colonial regime did not so much institutionalize capitalism as pillage. While classical capitalism can be dynamic and creative, pillage has no such potential. Even if the colonizers had been less inclined to rapacity, colonial capitalism would still have been incapable of liberating the productive forces in Africa because of the external orientation of the economy. Colonial capitalism was more interested in external demand than internal demand; it was not interested in turning the primary products into manufactured goods in the colonies, and thus the development of technology was inhibited. Finally, it was not interested in ploughing back capital into the colony; this was not conducive to economic growth.

Since independence, some of the regressive characteristics of capitalism in Africa have been reinforced much to the detriment of the prospects of economic growth. The reinforcement of these characteristics has to do with the situation of the ruling classes in Africa; particularly the disparity between their economic and political power. I have mentioned earlier that the African bourgeoisie has a very weak material base even in those countries such as Nigeria and Kenya where capitalism is more established and the process of class formation considerably advanced. I have also indicated that the weakness of the material base imperils the survival of the African bourgeoisie. The strengthening of its material base has naturally become one of the major preoccupations of this bourgeoisie. It is what it is doing about strengthening its material base that interests us for its actions in this regard are reinforcing the regressive characteristics of capitalism in Africa.

HOW THE AFRICAN BOURGEOISIE STRENGTHENS ITS MATERIAL BASE

If the African bourgeoisie is to strengthen its material base, then it must appropriate more of the surplus value which the labour of the rest of the population produces. African bourgeoisies must find more effective ways of exploitation in addition to the usual method of private capitalist exploitation. For this classic type of exploitation by entrepreneurs who hire wage-labour and realize surplus value, is restricted in Africa by the fact that only a very small proportion of the labour force is in wage employment. Thus this form of exploitation is not the dominant form of exploitation in Africa, as it is in many other parts of the world. While, however, it would be incorrect to conclude from the relatively low incidence of this form of exploitation and the weakness of the private sector that there are no classes in Africa, it is essential for African bourgeoisies to resort to subtler forms of exploitation.

One of these is the direct use of coercive power for expropriation. Something akin to what Marx describes as primitive accumulation is taking place all over Africa: the direct use of coercion to appropriate economic surplus or the means of production. Sometimes this is done under the cover of political conflict; some people are denounced for some political crime and then murdered or imprisoned and their property seized. Sometimes, it is done gangster style. Sometimes it is done under the cover of religious or ethnic conflict; a religious or ethnic group is denounced for being unpatriotic and subversive, or for economic exploitation of other groups, and popular hatred is built up against them. Then, under cover of this popular antipathy, the unfortunate group is abused, sometimes to a point amounting to genocide, and their property taken from them. Quite often it takes the form of direct class action. For instance many of the land registration and consolidation policies were a cover for depriving peasants of their land and for capitalizing agriculture.

The above is hardly a manner of accumulation conducive to the development of the forces of production. When primitive accumulation is carried out at the expense of peasants and workers it merely dramatizes the class contradictions of contemporary Africa and increases the mutual alienation of leaders and followers. This correspondingly reduces the ability of the leaders to mobilize the people and liberate their energy. When this process of primitive accumulation is directed against specific factions of the bourgeoisie or petty bourgeoisie, it is equally counter-productive. To begin with, those elements of the petty bourgeoisie or the bourgeoisie who are expropriated and/or liquidated by the politically hegemonic faction are likely to be the ones that have some entrepreneurial skill. To the extent that this assumption is correct, coercive accumulation depletes the small stock of people capable of making capitalism creative. More importantly, using violence to expropriate other members of the ruling class increases the level of insecurity within this class for everyone, including the hegemonic faction. This sets in motion a vicious circle of extremism and political violence. Insecurity makes political actors struggle even more grimly and tenaciously for political power and the high premium on political power inclines political actors to use any method which will produce desired results rather than confine themselves to methods of competition which are moral or legal. The further implication of all this is that everyone gets totally involved in the struggle for survival to the detriment of development. Under these conditions, neither culture nor industry can flourish. There is another sense in which development suffers. As the hegemonic faction of the ruling class successfully uses force to expropriate other factions of the ruling class as well as peasants and workers, the concentration of energy on politics is reinforced. In other words, this faction comes to feel even more strongly that what really counts is political power, that once one has political power one can have everything else —

including economic wealth. It reinforces the belief already current in Africa that wealth comes not by engaging in productive activity but by acquiring political power.

We have an interesting paradox. Coercive exploitation arises mainly out of the ruling class's insecure hold on political power, and the need to support it with a sound material base. But the use of state power to engage in coercive expropriation leads to an exaggerated importance of political power with consequences that actually retard the development of the material base. Of course the objective reality of the importance of economic power asserts itself. Indeed, the passion for political power underlines the importance of the material base, for, as we have seen, it is precisely the material base which is partly responsible for generating this passion. This reality asserts itself in an even more forceful way, namely the continued insecurity of the African ruling class. Despite its attempts at accumulation by coercive and other means, the contradictions of this situation have not permitted the African bourgeoisie much success in consolidating its material base. Its hold on power remains tenuous and its insecurity persists and may even increase. The high incidence of political violence in both intra-class and inter-class competition underlines this insecurity and the importance of the material base.

The third type of policy which the African bourgeoisie uses to bolster its material base is to apply political pressure on the imperialist agents operating in Africa for a greater share of the surplus. These pressures take many forms. The major form is to mobilize nationalist feelings against foreign capital and then insist on partnership with it. With few exceptions, this is really what the drive for indigenization in Africa amounts to. The case studies in the previous chapter have already shown how indigenization is not so much a dislodging of imperialism as accommodation and partnership with it.

Let us now look at how indigenization and the other policies used by the African bourgeoisie to put foreign capital under pressure affect the prospects of development. To begin with, the general tendency of these policies is to prevent the development of an indigenous bourgeoisie with entrepreneural skills, and to reinforce the divorce of the African bourgeoisie from production. In effect what these policies mean is that the African bourgeoisie interposes itself as a political middleman between international capital and the masses. What they offer in return for a greater share of surplus is political protection — the use of political power to curb labour unrest and control wages. They also promise to refrain from 'vindictive' restrictions on licences for foreign concerns, capital movements etc. In short, even as they penetrate the economic sphere to reinforce their material base, they specialize in the political aspects of this sphere, that is, in the political management of the conditions of production.

However, we have seen that in some cases indigenization and related policies have been directed not simply at extracting more surplus from international capital by offering political protection in return, but by compelling international capital to take elements of the African bourgeoisie into partnership. The partnership usually takes two forms. One is the acquisition of shares by Africans in foreign controlled enterprises. The acquisition of shares is often completed by increasing indigenous participation on the Board of Directors. The other type of partnership is the acquisition of shares by the government, often to the point where the government or 'the public' becomes the majority shareholder. These forms of partnership do not usually amount to very much as far as developing indigenous entrepreneural skill or involving the indigenous bourgeoisie in production is concerned. In the case of private ownership of shares the indigenous shareholders are usually 'sleeping partners' content to let foreign management get on with production and profit-making, and interested mainly in a good return on their investment. This is all the more so because those who buy into foreign business are people already employed in some other capacity. The case of public ownership is not much different. To begin with, those who act for the government in the new enterprise will generally be bureaucrats who do not normally possess entrepreneural skills or attempt to develop such skills. The actual management of production is generally left to the representatives of foreign capital. This trend is reinforced by the prevailing capitalist ethos, particularly commitment to profitability. Insofar as the government is anxious to make the enterprise profitable it tends to leave it to the management of the specialists in profit-making, the representatives of foreign capital. Foreign capital favours this arrangement and tries to ensure its perpetuation. Obviously its interest depends heavily on making itself indispensable. And it makes itself indispensable by jealously guarding its control of technology, by manipulating its entrepreneural skills and its links with the international market. Because of such monopoly, foreign capital can effectively control an enterprise and sustain its exploitative operations even when public ownership of equity exceeds 80%. It is not at all peculiar for multinational corporations with immense investment in Africa, such as Lonrho, to be quite happy with the new trend of public participation.

So the new partnership promises little indigenous control of production. It promises even less involvement of the African bourgeoisie in production and virtually no enhancement of their entrepreneurial skill. Most importantly, the new partnership and the other policies used by the African bourgeoisie to get a greater share of the surplus vis-a-vis international capital are not reducing dependence, or eliminating the exploitative links of dependence. Far from eliminating it, the partnership makes the situation safer for foreign capital by supporting it with political power. All this cannot help the battle against underdevelopment or the liberation of the forces of production in Africa.

I now turn to the fourth method which the African bourgeoisie is using to strengthen its material base, namely state capitalism. By state capitalism

I mean the accumulation of capital by the state. The state can be used by African bourgeoisies to accomplish this in various ways. One way which started in the colonial era involves state organs themselves using coercion to exact tribute from the population. In particular, the state extracts taxes from the people even when — notably in the rural areas — they get virtually nothing in return for the taxes they pay. A second common device and perhaps the most significant form of coercive exploitation by the state in terms of the quantity of the surplus involved, is government monopoly control over the marketing of primary commodities. Apart from the oil producing countries and a few other minor exceptions, African countries on average get about 70% of their export revenues from primary products. The state uses parastatal organizations such as marketing boards to control the export of these commodities. Peasants and farmers are obliged to sell to these boards or to approved intermediary institutions or individuals who in turn sell to these boards. The boards then sell to the overseas market. The exploitation in this procedure lies in the enormous difference between what the state pays to the producers and what it gets from the overseas buyers.

State capitalism today — and this is one of the most interesting developments of the post-colonial state — takes yet another form: the state itself acting as entrepreneur. While the colonial state was statist, its statism consisted in ubiquitous and heavyhanded control of economy and polity. The post-colonial state has extended statism to the entrepreneurial role. Why this change is taking place is quite easy to understand. The colonial government could afford to concentrate on exploitation to the exclusion of development. But the African government which replaced it could not afford to do so; for reasons that are too obvious to detain us. Once a commitment to economic development was made, the state had to assume an entrepreneurial role because it controlled such a large proportion of the society's surplus and because there was very little capital to mobilize for entrepreneurial activities in the private sector, except that part of it associated with international capitalism. Another important stimulus to the development of the state's entrepreneurial role was the weak material base of the African bourgeoisie. To strengthen this base, they had to go beyond the obvious option of using political power to appropriate a greater share of the surplus. They also had to create wealth, and state power was their major access to substantial capital, as well as the easiest.

Insofar as the state is acting as an entrepreneur, the actual mechanism of exploitation is, in many respects, the same as in the case of the individual capitalist. The state employee gives up the use value of his labour to the state in return for wages, and the state appropriates the value of the product of this labour in excess of its wages or cost of reproduction. Why not then assimilate state capitalism into the first type of exploitation ? Because that would obscure the singular importance of this capitalist role of the state. The fact that it is the state rather than individual capitalists which is exploiting workers, has notable consequences for the visibility of exploitation, the development of capitalism, the distribution of surplus, not to mention the character of the class struggle.

In Africa state capitalism has been associated both with the state founding new enterprises and with the extension of the state's control over the economy in other ways. This extension usually takes the form of nationalization. The resources which thus come under state control are mobilized and used as capital by the state acting as entrepreneur. What was said about the new partnership between the African bourgeoisie and international capital applies to the policy of nationalization. With few exceptions nationalization amounts merely to one concrete manifestation of the new partnership. Here again the African bourgeoisie largely confines itself to a political role, the role of providing political protection — partly because it lacks entrepreneurial skills and partly because it has no interest in provoking a breach with international capital. Generally, nationalization does very little to reduce the influence of the agents of foreign capital, influence which they are able to exercise by their control of technology, by skills in management and marketing etc.

More importantly, state capitalism is a regressive form of capitalism. This point should not be difficult to grasp if one is careful not to confuse state capitalism with statism or with state control of the economy or state involvement in enterprises. When one talks of state capitalism, one presupposes the class cleavage of bourgeoisie and proletariat and the antagonism between capital and labour. Further, one presupposes that while production may be more or less social, appropriation will be largely private. What distinguishes state capitalism from the orthodox capitalism of the *Wealth of Nations* is its monopoly character. It is a peculiarly coercive monopoly. For instance, state capitalism entails coercive monopolization of capital, of markets etc.

The regressive character of state capitalism is inherent in the distortions brought about by its monopoly character. State capitalism is scarcely dynamic since it usually fails to make the contributions which competition for the market, via a better and better input/output ratio, can make to efficiency, expansion and technological innovation. It is also regressive in the sense that it is a form of capitalism which involves no risks, demands no imagination and sets no performance standards. It involves no risks because the bourgeoisie is not using its own capital but the resources of the public, and because state capitalism is typically directed at those forms of economic activity which are by their very nature highly profitable. And it is because it involves no risk that it demands no imagination and sets no standards. This is why state capitalism is not conducive to the rapid development of productive forces.

I will conclude this section by raising one objection to the case that the African bourgeoisie's attempts to reinforce its material base are not conducive to the development of productive forces and the overcoming of

underdevelopment. The objection is as follows: irrespective of the immediate effect of these measures on the development of the productive forces,
they are nevertheless the essential preliminary for such development.
Capital has to be concentrated before capitalist development can take place.
The measures in question help us to concentrate capital, to create a real
capitalist class which will eventually engineer capitalist development.

This argument is unsound. The measures under consideration have not
done very much to expand the capitalist class or even strengthen substantially the material base of the bourgeoisie as a class. Even though members
of the African bourgeoisie are aware of the weakness of their material base
and the necessity of strengthening it, it cannot be presumed that they will
rationally go about rectifying this weakness. Quite the contrary. The
pursuit of this objective will be mediated and distorted by the contradictions within the bourgeoisie, possibly to an extent that will largely defeat
the original purpose. Individuals and factions within the class will think
primarily of their particular interests, not of the collective interest of the
class, and will act accordingly. Thus, opportunities for strengthening the
material base of the class inevitably become occasions for inter-personal
and inter-faction competition and to some extent defeat the collective
interest. But these are generalities. The question is whether circumstances
in the African situation are such that this self-defeat might be said to be
occurring ? All the measures which the African bourgeoisie is taking to
strengthen its material base tend to increase the level of political competition within this class. Coercive appropriation and accumulation under-
taken primarily by the hegemonic faction of the bourgeoisie worries the
other factions some of whose members inevitably become victims of the
process. The attempt to pressure international capital into giving up a
greater share of the surplus is made in the context of contradictions such
as those between the comprador elements as against more national elements
within the bourgeoisie. Inevitably it has a differential impact on the
fortunes of the various factions and generates anxieties. Finally, nationalization of resources and state capitalism have enormous potential for
increasing the power of the hegemonic faction of the bourgeoisie as well as
for weakening non-hegemonic factions. In short, these measures reveal,
deepen and politicize the contradictions within the bourgeoisie and increase
the premium on winning the intra-class competition. Under these circumstances even the hegemonic faction of the bourgeoisie will not be thinking
primarily of the collective good of the class. This is how it comes about
that the purpose of strengthening the material base of the bourgeoisie is
largely defeated. More specifically, it is defeated because in the heat of
competition the hegemonic faction tries to restrict the access of the other
factions to the accumulation of capital. Expanded opportunity for accumulation and stringent restrictions of access to accumulation combine to
produce monopoly — monopoly of economic and political power by the
hegemonic faction. In the meantime, the grim anxiety and struggle within

the bourgeoisie reinforce its regressive tendencies. People look for quick wealth, and corruption grows. Everyone goes for mobile assets, capital is salted away overseas, and so on. I will now turn to the third and final aspect of the relationship between underdevelopment and the dynamics of class relations in Africa.

DEPOLITICIZATION: THE AFRICAN BOURGEOISIE'S RESPONSE TO REVOLUTIONARY PRESSURES

There are strong revolutionary pressures in Africa: pressures against the maintenance of the existing exploitative class relations and hence pressures against the very survival of the African bourgeoisie. These pressures arise from: (a) the desperate poverty of the African masses; (b) the sharp and highly visible differences between the rich and the poor; (c) rising expectations associated with 'modernization'; (d) the example of developed countries, made even more effective by their penetration of the periphery; (e) the politicization of the popular consciousness by the nationalist movement and by the dynamics of contradictions between the metropolitan bourgeoisie and the African bourgeoisie.

I will not elaborate on these pressures here. What interests me is not an account of these pressures but how the African bourgeoisie is reacting to them. Their options are limited to two broad strategies. One is to meet the demands inherent in these pressures. There are two kinds of demands involved here. One is the demand for equality which, carried to its logical conclusion, is a demand for the abolition of the bourgeoisie and its privileges. The African bourgeoisie obviously cannot meet this demand. What it can do and what it is doing is to make some token gestures such as introducing slightly more egalitarian taxation and having government officials use more modest cars etc. The African bourgeoisie will make marginal changes in the area of distribution without touching the core of the problem of inequality, which lies in the realm of production relations and which can be dealt with ultimately only by revolutionizing production relations. So equality is ruled out because the demand for equality cannot be met without a socialist revolution which the ruling class will not sponsor. The second kind of demand made by the masses is only a little less difficult for the bourgeoisie to meet; it is the demand for social well-being, for easing the agony of extreme want. Even this demand cannot be met except in some marginal ways, since the very conditions of underdevelopment very drastically limit the expansion of the economic surplus. Even if the existing surplus were distributed more fairly, it would not make much difference. But the existing surplus will not be fairly distributed in the context of existing class contradictions.

That leaves the African bourgeoisie with the other broad strategy of discouraging these demands, and preventing their political manifestation and radicalization. That is what the African bourgeoisie is doing. Its strategy is depoliticization. Depoliticization entails reducing the effective participation of the masses and of non-hegemonic factions of the ruling class, and preventing some interests and points of view from finding political expression. The point of reducing the effective political partici-pation of the masses is to render them impotent, to prevent the political system from being overloaded with demands which are not conducive to its survival and to render the masses less available for socialization into radical political or oppositional behaviour by non-hegemonic factions of the ruling class. By preventing certain interests and opinions from finding political expression, the ruling class expects to obtain a level of political unity out of proportion to existing contradictions in the material base, and to reduce the possibility of harnessing the antipathies towards the political and economic system into a strong revolutionary force.

The process of depoliticization has made African countries political monoliths. Every African country is in effect a one-party state in the sense that every regime in Africa assumes its exclusive right to rule and prohibits organized opposition. Military regimes are in this respect similar to one-party systems. Most importantly, the process of depoliticization has made the African politics particularly brutal. Given the contradictions in contem-porary African society, depoliticization cannot be carried out without brutal repression.

The one-party system is as much a tool for asserting the exclusive claims of the hegemonic faction within the new bourgeoisie as it is an instrument for disenfranchising the masses. Ironically insofar as depoli-ticization is necessary for maintaining the existing exploitative production relations, the hegemonic faction of the bourgeoisie which depoliticizes opposing factions is expressing the objective interests of these factions as a class even when it represses them. Even those factions of the exploiting class (such as those associated with the cultural apparatus of the state) who seem to have the least to gain by depoliticization will be obliged to engage in depoliticization if they become hegemonic. Two conclusions which follow from this are noteworthy. First, depoliticization within the exploit-ing class is only partially an effect of the struggle for power within this class; it is primarily a necessary condition for the maintenance of the class as a whole vis-a-vis the exploited class. Second, the popular assumption that return to civilian rule will significantly affect the incidence of political repression is altogether mistaken.

The effects of the process of depoliticizing the exploiting class are very complex. Insofar as this process helps to maintain the existing class structure, it might be said to promote political stability. Political stability is used here to refer to the persistence of the political structure, particu-larly the relationship of the dominant and subordinate systems of roles which express the class situation politically. While enhancing political stability in this way, depoliticization of the exploiting class tendentially accentuates governmental instability. Governmental instability describes a state of affairs in which the control of governmental institutions changes hands often and in an erratic manner. There is a sense, however, in which this process of depoliticization of the exploiting class promotes governmental stability. It does so insofar as it leads to the homogenization of the exploiting class. Depoliticization increases homogenization by imposing ideological unity, by building alliances between factions, by co-opting dangerous opponents into the hegemonic faction and by liquidating certain other factions altogether. Nevertheless, it would seem that, on balance, this intra-class depoliticization is more conducive to governmental instability than to stability. This is so mainly because it greatly reinforces the destabilizing effect which statism produces, by focussing the ambitions of all the factions of the exploiting class primarily on the capture of state power, by making the outcome of the struggle for hegemony among the factions of the bourgeoisie too important. The process of depoliticization intensifies these tendencies, because in effect it constitutes an attack by the hegemonic faction on the particularism of others, and even on their survival. This attack on particularism is all the more threatening because it seeks to abolish political particularism without abolishing (at least in the short term) the objective conditions of this particularism. Even when this attack succeeds, and something like a one-party system emerges, governmental instability remains, and perhaps increases. For the major effect of the one-party system is to compress the arena of struggle without reducing the objective basis of the differences between the factions. Thus pressure mounts, and explosions occur periodically. When major differences in this political monolith appear, a crisis invariably occurs. The options for resolving these differences are drastically limited. It usually comes down to suppressing either the leaders or those challenging them. Since in the one-party system it is rarely possible to remove the leaders by following the rules, they are removed in spite of the rules, just as the opposition is brutalized in spite of the rules.

DEPOLITICIZATION AND THE PERPETUATION OF UNDERDEVELOPMENT

I now want to consider the consequences of depoliticization for the prospects of development. First, depoliticization reduces the prospect of overcoming underdevelopment by facilitating the ascendancy of the elements of the ruling class associated with the coercive machinery of the state. As we have seen, depoliticization entails massive repression which in turn leads to the enlargement of the role of the coercive institutions, especially the army and the police. Thus the bulk of African countries are governed by military governments or by civilian regimes so heavily dependent on the army that they are for all practical purposes merely agents of the men in uniform. The ascendancy of the specialists of coercion reinforces an unfortunate tendency which already exists in Africa, the tendency towards booty capitalism, which is not conducive to development — not even capitalist development. The point is easy enough to see. The weapon available to the new rulers for both political and economic competition is force. There is therefore a tendency to apply force ubiquitously in political and economic competition and also to appropriate surplus by force. Admittedly the dialectics of the situation will tend to mitigate this booty capitalism and transform it to something more like orthodox capitalism in the very long run. For the men in uniform soon accumulate and to some extent become exploiters by class situation. If indeed this were to happen, and quickly, it would be fortunate for Africa because orthodox capitalism is clearly far more conducive to economic growth than booty capitalism.

Unfortunately, we cannot posit a quick end to this phase of booty capitalism despite the tendency for the military to use instruments of violence to become capitalists proper (i.e. exploiters by class situation). The military itself is riddled with class contradictions. When the military comes to power, only the top leadership of its structure is able to accumulate substantially. Of course the demands of survival will encourage the upper strata to ensure that some rewards are passed down to the lower strata. Despite such prudent gestures, distribution will reflect differential effective control of the means of production. The lower military strata will strive to get to the top and when they do so others will strive to remove them. Insofar as the top military leadership accumulate and become capitalists proper, they intensify the desire of the lower strata to seize power and to increase their share of the booty. When the new coup occurs, movement away from booty capitalism is interrupted and the system regresses to booty capitalism. Thus the movement away from booty capitalism tends to negate itself.

The depoliticization of society expresses and brings into clear relief the alienation of the masses from their rulers. Having rendered the masses irrelevant except as payers of tribute, the process thereby excludes the possibility of mobilizing them and releasing their energies for development. This is perhaps the greatest setback to development; circumstances do not permit the tapping of the most valuable resource of a country, the energy of its people. All the talk about mobilization of the peasantry and primary emphasis on the development of the rural areas 'where most of our people live' leads nowhere. Not because the leaders have no interest in rural development, nor because of shortage of capital, lack of technology or the conservatism of peasants, but because, given the class situation, rural development policies will necessarily have an exploitative thrust and such policies will elicit a grudging performance at best.

To sum up, we have seen how the class structure of Africa constitutes an obstacle to development, even capitalist development, in Africa. By impeding development the class structure generates its own dialectical negation for, as we have seen, the persistence of underdevelopment especially extreme poverty in Africa is a source of strong revolutionary pressures.

4

IDEOLOGICAL CONTAINMENT
AND ITS CONTRADICTIONS

Our analysis of the dynamics of social forces in Africa and in the international system indicates that the African bourgeoisie is unable significantly to develop productive forces or bring about even capitalist economic growth. We have seen that this inability is highly detrimental to the survival of the African bourgeoisie especially as economic stagnation only radicalizes revolutionary pressures already inherent in societies which suffer from underdevelopment and class divisions. In the last chapter we saw how the African bourgeoisie is trying to cope with this difficulty through a strategy of depoliticization. In what follows, I wish to examine a very different strategy used, namely ideological management of the problem through the bourgeoisie propagating an apparently more progressive ideology — a process I describe as defensive radicalism. This aspect of the bourgeoisie's reaction is important and interesting because it throws light on the development of social forces and on the necessity as well as the possibility of socialism in Africa; it also sheds light on the relation between consciousness and existence.

This particular type of ideological management which the African bourgeoisie has 'chosen' is itself a product of social forces. However, it is not merely a wholly dependent variable because it also modifies the operating forces. And it modifies them — albeit unintentionally — in such a way as to make them more conducive to the radicalization of popular consciousness. This is the process that will be examined here. In order to reveal very clearly the relation between existential conditions and consciousness, and to appreciate more fully which — socialism or capitalism — has the better prospects in Africa, we have to go back in time to the colonial period. Starting with this period, I will show how changing existential conditions are related to changing consciousness and how the dynamics of social forces push the African bourgeoisie to radicalize the popular consciousness in a manner that is ultimately inimical to the maintenance of existing capitalist production relations in Africa.

I begin by considering colonial economy and colonial ideology. As I indicated before, colonial capitalism was a unique form of capitalism. It was not based on the principle of laisser-faire although it was not without some elements of this principle. Rather it was based on explicit rejection of the notion of consumer sovereignty (for the indigenous people, at any rate) and frank acceptance of the necessity for authoritative allocation of work and of rewards.

These were not arbitrary modifications. They were imposed by the logic of colonialism. To begin with, the drive for colonies was dictated by the need to avoid wasteful competition and to secure sources of raw materials which could be completely monopolized. Since colonialism was such a massive pillage of the human and natural resources of the colonized peoples, aggression and hostility permeated, vitiated and indeed defined the relationship between colonizer and colonized. Without coercion the equilibrium of the colonial system would have been destroyed. In the colonial economy, force became the key instrument of the profit motive. Force was used to allocate roles, force was used to ensure the supply of labour, and force was used to extract and allocate the economic surplus.

The colonial political system was necessarily as unilateral as the colonial economic system. Consumer sovereignty could not be denied in the economic sphere and tolerated in the political sphere, because to allow it in the political realm would trigger an irresistible pressure for allowing it in the economic sphere.

THE IDEOLOGY OF COLONIALISM

The logic of colonial relations and the concrete interest inherent in these relations determine the dominant ideology of the colonial system. It is customary to make much of the differences between the colonial practices and ideologies of the Portuguese, Belgians, French, Germans, English, Italians and Spaniards. We have been sufficiently impressed by these distinctions that we now talk about enlightened colonizers and unenlightened ones; those who took their *mission civilisatrice* seriously and those who merely exploited. The fact of the matter is that colonialism, as an objective relation, demands — indeed imposes — a particular political system and particular ideologies concordant with its objective character. Thus, all colonizers used essentially the same ideology. They all developed very similar justification for colonialism, from the same premises, namely that colonialism was beneficial to the colonized in the fundamental sense of improving the quality of their lives. Colonialism became, not self-seeking, not exploitation, but salvation. The very terminology that the colonizers used to describe colonialism reflected the substance of their ideology. Thus they described the colonies as 'protectorates', implying that the colonial power was really fiduciary and that its *raison d'etre* was protection of the colonies. The British often preferred to think of colonialism as a 'mandate' to help backward peoples, the French and Portuguese and Belgians thought of it as a civilizing mission or 'tutelage'.

Such characterization of colonialism not only had the effect of making it look like generosity instead of rapacity, but it also enabled the colonizers to develop some defence against the charge that colonialism was racist or that colonization entailed treating the colonized peoples as subhuman, for this characterization of colonialism presupposes the possibility of civilizing the colonized people and hence their potential for cultural existence. Of course, one could not pretend that the colonized are civilized, or equal to everyone else. Existing realities could not be ignored. The colonized had to be treated in a manner commensurate with their stage of development as men and this unfortunately meant limiting their participation and their claims in the community of civilized men temporarily. However, the important thing is that the obstacles in the way of their development were removable, and colonialism ensured their removal. So, with uncanny ingenuity, the colonizers were able to reconcile racism with the proclamation of the equality of all men.

The ideology of the colonizers complemented the political economy of colonialism very well. It justified the system in terms of its benefits to the exploited without in any way compelling any mitigation of the harshness and the brutality of the exploitation. Every assault on the colonized could be defended as a necessary concession to the realities of his state of development. In the meantime, the assault on his way of life and on his dignity became the tool for creating these very 'realities'. In other words, the systematic brutalization of the colonized became the very instrument for reducing him to a subhuman existence, the condition of existence he would have to be in to deserve colonization. Thus, somehow, the more inhuman the practice of colonialism, the more plausible its ideology.

THE COLONIAL ECONOMY AND THE IDEOLOGY OF NATIONALISM

We have looked at one side of the coin. We have seen the congruence between the ideology of the colonizers and their objective interests. We must now look at the other side of the colonial relation — the colonized. What is the relation of the thinking of the nationalist leaders to their objective situation and what are the implications of this relation ?

To answer this question we must begin by noting the link between the nationalist movement and the contradictions of the colonial economy. One major source of contradiction was the economy's supply of labour. The colonizers needed labour to carry out the exploitation of the colony: roads and railways had to built, a bureaucratic network had to be established, men were needed to gather the raw materials and to prepare them for export, and domestic servants were needed for commodious living. The colonial economy had to obtain labour from a subject population that was not integrated into a monetary economy. The supply of labour could not be left to the usual market mechanism. Coercion had to be used. People were simply rounded up and forced to work; a 'money' tax was imposed in order to compel people to enter the money economy. These measures deepened the antipathies between the colonizers and the colonized.

Virtually every policy which the colonizers devised to facilitate their economic exploitation recreated the same contradictions. Consider the education policy. Some basic education was necessary to ensure an adequate supply of labour. The colonizers offered the most elementary liberal education with a heavy religious bias. A minimum of technical and scientific education was offered because colonial domination owed much to the mystique of the colonizer's technological and scientific superiority. Religious education was emphasized because it was considered an excellent vehicle for indoctrinating the colonized with a cult of subservience. This educational programme carried its own contradictions. To begin with, education, however basic, carried with it the threat of the colonized penetrating the colonizer's world, and the more the mystery of his power was penetrated, the more its spell was weakened. The concentration on liberal education may have protected the colonizer's monopoly of science and technology, but that was small consolation, given the fact that liberal education led to the discovery of Western liberal ideas and to the development of political consciousness and the skills needed for political effectiveness. Liberal education generated an indigenous leadership and equipped them with a common language. It helped create the conditions for eradicating colonialism.

The colonizer's quest for economies of scale led to similar contradictions. The search for economies of scale led to the geographical concentration of economic activities and subsequently to the concentration of the wretched victims of colonialism. They were concentrated geographically, subjected to a common life style and given a new common consciousness. To make colonialism more profitable this army of labourers was denied any welfare scheme. Eventually the people relied on their own ingenuity to set up an elaborate and sophisticated network of tribal and secondary associations. These associations provided scholarships, loans and succour for orphans, widows, the aged and the unemployed. They became an alternative social service system. More importantly they provided the nationalist movements with leadership training and a ready-made network of political organizations to build on. Those who are familiar with the contemporary history of Africa know that most of the nationalist parties in Africa grew from these associations.

We have seen how the colonial situation had a latent tendency to evolve towards its own dialectical negation. We have seen how the contradictions of the situation created the national movements and their leadership. The leaders of the nationalist movements had fundamental common interests. They derived status from their proximity to the colonizer's culture. They had a vested interest in the colonizer's value system and in preserving some of their links with the colonizer's economy. They had an interest in keeping the nationalist revolution limited, to ensure the preservation of

privilege. They were the ones who would benefit most from the displace-
ment of the colonial regime for they would inherit economic and political
power. Let us look at how the nationalist leaders acted and how they
thought in order to see whether they were thinking as a group in their
historical situation.

To begin with, let us look at their political stance. The political stance
and the political style of both the colonizers and the nationalist leaders
was rigidly defined by the colonial situation. As has been pointed out, the
relation between colonizer and colonized was one permeated by profound
antagonism. The capitalism of colonialism, booty capitalism, did not offer
much scope for compromise. The single issue of booty capitalism was
simply the possibility of its maintenance. And this issue resolved itself into
the balance of power between colonizer and colonized. In the political
sphere there was the same brutal simplicity. The colonizers could not
maintain or expect to maintain their presence and their exploitation by
the consent of their victims. It was clear that whatever else they may have
done to maintain their presence, force was ultimately the basis of their
claim. So in the final analysis, the question of the survival of the colonial
polity was a question of the maintenance of a balance of power which
favoured the colonizers. The colonizers were under pressure to monopolize
power and to render the colonized powerless. One could not be a colonizer
and a democrat at the same time. If the colonizers allowed popular
participation in government, colonialism would automatically end. However much the colonizer professed his commitment to democracy and thus
to the political development of his victims, the primary goal of his politics
was the exclusion of the subject population from power — though not
necessarily from token participation. For their part, the leaders of the
nationalist movements found that they too were obliged to take an uncom-
promising political stance. They had to make an exclusive claim to government in the name of the people and to deny that the colonizers had any
claim at all to government. If they had simply sought to share power or to
ameliorate their political status, or to stand for more enlightened and more
effective government, they would have implicitly legitimated the colonial
regime. Therein lies the brutal simplicity of colonial politics: one exclusive
claim to power against another. The politics aptly complemented the
economic relation.

The leaders of nationalist movements used essentially the same ideology
to support their struggle. Let us examine the major characteristics of this
ideology. One aspect of this ideology was the rehabilitation of the self-
respect of the colonized people. All the nationalist leaders including the
ones who were the most impregnated with the colonial mentality engaged
in such rehabilitation. The objective necessity of this element in the
ideology of the nationalist is fairly obvious. The colonizer faced the problem of justifying the plunder of their victims' resources and their assault
on their way of life. When all the equivocations are done away with, their

defence amounted to the claim that their victims were somewhat less than human — indeed the whole point of the civilizing mission was to make them human. Colonial politics then set out to turn their victims into what they would have to be to deserve the treatment they got; hence the systematic humiliation and the denigration of their culture and history. The maintenance of colonialism depended very much on the ability of the colonizer to make his claim to superiority plausible and on the acquiescence of the colonized in their representation as inferior. The people could not be mobilized into colonial politics and they could not effectively wage war against colonialism as long as they were burdened by a sense of inferiority. In these circumstances the ideologies of anti-colonialism had to reflect the necessity of restoring the self-respect of the colonized. This involved the rehabilitation of the history and culture of Africa, and the assertion of the uniqueness and vitality of the African mind and of African institutions, as implicit in the concepts of Negritude, the African personality, and African socialism. We find these themes in such writings as Senghor's *African Socialism*, Kenyatta's *Facing Mount Kenya*, Azikiwe's *Renascent Africa*, Nkrumah's *I Speak of Freedom*.

The second component of the nationalist ideology was the denigration of colonial rule. There is a sense in which this component was merely an aspect of the restoration of the self-respect of the colonized. But it was more than this. It was necessary to reveal the evil of colonialism in its totality and enormity in order to fight it most effectively. So without exception, the nationalist leaders tore at the mystifications of colonialism and tried to show how it had vitiated and impoverished its victims.

The third component of the nationalist ideology was the assertion of self-determination. There is no need to show the objective necessity of this component. Colonialism being what it is, to oppose colonialism in anything other than a trivial sense is to assert the right of self-determination. The demand for self-determination was inherent in the basic contradiction of the colonial situation.

The fourth component of the ideology of the nationalist leadership was the doctrine of liberal democracy. The leaders of the nationalist movements in Africa were liberal democrats. This seems somewhat surprising because liberal democracy was the ideology of the colonizers whose culture the nationalist movement was supposed to be rejecting wholesale. It is surprising also because liberal democracy was the political correlate of capitalism and the colonization of Africa was a logical outcome of West European capitalism. But if we look at the situation and the interests of the leaders of the nationalist movements in Africa, their resort to the doctrine of liberal democracy is natural, indeed inevitable. The choice of this doctrine was due to its accessibility and utility. The compelling reason for the adoption of the liberal ideology was its utility. First, it was useful for mobilizing liberal opinion in the metropolitan countries. It was most effective to appeal to Western liberals in terms of values and doctrines they understood and accepted. Second, it was the ideological correlate of the capitalist relations of production which the nationalist leaders intended to retain and have retained. Finally, and most importantly, liberal ideology was the classic tool for coping with the fundamental contradiction of all bourgeois revolutions, which is as follows. On the one hand, the bourgeoisie had to appeal to the principle of self-determination in order to gain mass support to defeat feudalists (as in the case of the French and English revolutions), or imperialists (as in the case of the American revolution and the Asian and African nationalist revolutions). On the other hand, class interests, especially as concretized in the relations of production, had to be defended. And this meant that popular sovereignty could not be allowed. For popular sovereignty or substantive democracy could not be allowed without eventually undermining the capitalist mode of production. Those who have read the classic statements of the ideology of liberal democracy such as Locke's *Second Treatise on Government*, Mill's *Essay on Liberty*, Bentham's *Representative Government*, Rousseau's *Social Contract*, and *The Declaration of the Rights of Man and of the Citizen* will be familiar with the way that liberal democracy has met this dilemma. The African nationalist leaders simply adapted the solution they found in these theories to their situation. They harped on the necessity of self-determination and on the virtues of democracy, equality and the dignity of man. But these brave words were perfectly safe because in the colonial situation, the substantive issue was alien rule and the substantive conception of self-determination would inevitably amount to the overthrow of alien rule. So they could talk about self-determination without any commitment to democracy, equality or the dignity of man. That they did not take these ideas seriously was soon apparent from their performance as the leaders of the new indigenous governments. However they had already betrayed their indifference to these ideals even before independence by their very vagueness and by their unconcern for the political consequences of the capitalist mode of production.

These are the four themes which constitute the core of the political ideology of African leaders. There is no African nationalist leader whose political ideology was not built on one or more of those four themes. We have seen then that in developing their political ideologies, African nationalist leaders were simply responding logically to the realities of their existence.

They thought as a group, at least in the sense that their thinking was fundamentally the same and congruent with the similarities of their objective situation.

I ought to mention that there were differences from one nationalist movement to another. But I am not sure that these differences are sufficiently important to detain us here. However one type of difference deserves mention since it is perhaps the only one of substantive significance; the difference between the countries ruled by a petty bourgeoisie oriented

towards socialism and the rest of Africa. I am thinking particularly of
Guinea-Bissau, Angola and Mozambique, where nationalist liberation was
pursued in association with a socialist ideology. I will return to the
question of differences later; at this point, all that need be said is that for
the period of the colonial struggle the ideological differences between these
countries and those of the rest of Africa are remarkably small. This is
easily ascertained by comparing for instance Cabral's *Revolution in Guinea*
with Nyerere's *Ujamaa* and *Freedom and Unity*, Nnamdi Azikiwe's
Renascent Africa and Nkrumah's *I Speak of Freedom*. The major difference
is that the progressive leaders such as Samora Machel have a clear, Marxist-
oriented analysis of imperialism, whereas the reactionary leaders such as
Azikiwe, Nkrumah, Kenyatta and Nyerere tend to substitute idealist
phraseology such as 'colonial oppression' for 'imperialism' and offer no
analysis of imperialism. One cannot really make too much of this because
everyone was fighting an occupying power and this blunted the differences
between progressives and reactionaries since it did not permit much
attention to be paid to internal class contradictions. The reactionary
leaders could talk of imperialism without inviting too much danger to
themselves. Another difference is that the leadership of countries such as
Angola made less of liberal ideology. But then, they too had to talk of
freedom, self-determination and popular sovereignty — concepts which
liberals use without concreteness. The ideology of a movement against a
colonizing power could not really avoid using these terms. The fact that
it was a people whose freedom was at issue would largely blur differences
between progressives interested in concrete freedom and reactionaries
interested only in abstract freedom. So to say that there was really not
much difference between the ideologies of countries such as Kenya and
Mozambique during the nationalist phase is not to impugn the revolutionary credentials of the latter. It is merely a recognition of the sameness
of the realities of the colonial situation.

IDEOLOGY IN THE POST COLONIAL ERA

When political independence came, the interests of the nationalist
leaders who inherited power changed somewhat, and their ideas and
dispositions to action changed correspondingly. The change from being an
oppositional group to being the governing authority was full of perils as
well as exciting possibilities. Authority had to be consolidated. The
appetite for participation and better welfare which the nationalist leaders
had excited had to be satisfied. The oppositional political orientation
which the nationalist struggle had produced had to be changed. With the
common enemy no longer formally in power, the problem of integration
loomed large.

These problems quickly revealed the contradictions within the newly independent society, particularly the contradiction between the new rulers and the masses. Consider, firstly, the politicization of the masses and the pressure for democratic participation which the nationalist struggle had created. If the new rulers chose to allow democracy in substance as opposed to appearance, they would have had to abolish the capitalist relations of production which they had inherited, for such relations of production are diametrically opposed to substantive democracy. So the choice was between denying the demand for participation and changing the relations of production. Consider, secondly, the question of the demand for material improvement of the masses. Colonial exploitation, neo-colonialism and other factors prevented the economies of the newly independent states from immediately generating goods and services of the magnitude necessary to satisfy the expectations of the people. So in the short run, the road to significant betterment of the material conditions of the masses really depended on the abolition of exploitative economic relations and on redistribution of resources. It is clear that the new rulers could not meet the pressure for participation or the demand for welfare in a manner compatible with the maintenance of existing relations of production and their own class privileges. And insofar as they could not solve these two problems, they were in no position to solve the problems of authority and integration.

The reaction of the new rulers was all that could reasonably be expected of anyone in their situation. They decided to maintain the exploitative relations and a stratification system which they dominated. They decided to firmly discourage demands for redistribution of wealth and for mass participation. Having made these commitments, they were obliged to use coercion to solve the problems of authority and integration and to initiate the process of depoliticization. The latter has been analysed in the previous chapter. As for coercion, all over Africa the masses were deprived of effective political participation; they are allowed — sometimes compelled — to vote in elections but their participation is inconsequential. Elections have become a redundant formality all over Africa. Dissident groups, counter-elites and progressives are intimidated, incarcerated or murdered. Workers' movements are deprived of all autonomy and effectiveness.

These are the realities that have now led to a hasty revision of the ideology of the nationalist leaders presently in power. If we compare the speeches and writings of the nationalist leaders before independence and after, we find that they all revised their ideologies along the following lines. Firstly, their ideology now proclaims the end of internal ideological conflict. It is argued that the problems facing the nation are clear, that everyone should apply himself to the task. In effect, the leaders of Africa are reducing politics to administration insofar as questions are no longer to be asked regarding the overriding goals of society and the legitimacy of the existing political and economic order. Secondly, emphasis has shifted from liberty to order. They argue that order (in effect, conformism) is necessary for maximum effectiveness in dealing with the problems of development. Order has to be maintained to discourage the numerous enemies who have designs on the independence of the new state. The institutionalized disorder so characteristic of Western politics is absolutely contrary to the African tradition. The African tradition of unanimity has to be rehabilitated because it is a more efficient and more civilized way of conducting public affairs. This argument becomes generalized as an argument against dissent, interest articulation and democratic participation, a defence of the monolithic political structure that is being created. Thirdly, the significance of independence is redefined to conceal the poor performance and self-interested behaviour of the ruling class. Since they are unwilling to change existing relations of production and redistribute available resources in a radically egalitarian direction and since constraints on their economies rule out any rapid increase of the economic surplus in the short run, they cannot hope to increase the material well-being of the masses as expected. So they now argue that the immediate significance of independence is hard work, not self-indulgence. Legitimate expectations of material betterment of the masses are now represented as naive, subversive or as reprehensible hedonism. The fourth characteristic of the post-independence ideologies is the emphasis on unity. This characteristic does not represent any change of trend because the pre-independence ideology had also placed stress on unity. In both the pre-independence and the post-independence periods the stress on unity served the same purpose, namely to cover up the contradictions in the society. In the period of the nationalist struggle, unity was associated with justice. In fact, the struggle for justice was the rationale of unity. The victims of colonialism needed to unite in order to combat their exploitation. In the post-independence era, the rulers use the idea of unity in a manner that is blatantly self-serving. African leaders are now calling for unity without reference to the justice of the relevant order. Indeed they do not even tolerate questions concerning the justice of existing order. At the same time the injustice of the status quo has emerged more clearly as the problems of the post-independence era reveal and deepen the contradictions between leaders and masses. Fifthly, aspects of the metropolitan bourgeoisies' ideology of development are adopted. We have already discussed what has been adopted and why. Sixthly, and most importantly, African leaders are responding to the revolutionary pressures from below with what I call, for lack of a better term, defensive radicalism. All the other characteristics are merely elements developing in the context of a strong and general thrust towards defensive radicalism and are defined and limited by this radicalism. This is why defensive radicalism deserves special attention.

DEFENSIVE RADICALISM AS AN IDEOLOGICAL PLOY

What is defensive radicalism ? It is an attempt at mystification. It is the assumption of a radical posture and the use of this posture as a cover for containing revolutionary pressures and for maintaining the status quo. There is no African country which is not involved in defensive radicalism which is manifested in the following tendencies: (a) the increasingly radical rhetoric against imperialism even among the most reactionary African leaderships such as those of the Ivory Coast, Senegal and Liberia; (b) the radical rhetoric of the Organization of African Unity against the continued colonization of Southern Africa; (c) the verbal commitment of most African leaders to some form of socialism and the rejection of capitalism; (d) the policy statements used to justify extensions of public ownership; (e) the militant attack on inequality in some African countries; (f) the policy statements explaining the curbs on the operations of foreign capital; (g) the show of being friendly with socialist countries such as Cuba. These are only a few examples.

It may be said that while these examples might vindicate the claim that certain African leaders are indeed increasingly taking a radical stance, they do not support the claim that this stance does not reflect a genuine radicalism and is merely one being taken to preserve the status quo. Fair enough. It would be useless to psychologize the problem and start thinking purely of motives. But we can draw reasonable conclusions from a comparison of words and deeds, and by following the logic of objective conditions. By these criteria it is not so difficult to show that defensive radicalism is taking place. Before going any further into the problem, however, it is desirable to consider separately those few African countries, such as Angola and Guinea-Bissau, where the petty bourgeoisie does not seem to have aspirations of becoming a bourgeoisie.

In the case of this handful of progressive countries, it is rather more difficult to say if and when defensive radicalism is occurring. These countries have less use for defensive radicalism and have taken substantive steps toward socialism. Even then, there are telling discrepancies. The radicalism of ideology outstrips the radicalism of their practice. By giving the impression that they are already socialist they in effect commit the sin of mystification, thereby perpetuating a status quo that amounts only to *Gotha Programme* socialism. They have been attacking inequality largely as a problem of the sphere of distribution rather than a problem rooted in the sphere of production, with all that that implies.

Having said all this the fact remains that these countries have clearly demonstrated the seriousness of their intention to move towards socialism. It may well be that the disparities between ideology and practice such as those we have pointed out are due not so much to an intention to mystify but to the pressures of the objective situation. Their policy could be a forced tactical compromise rather than defensive radicalism. As I said before, it is not easy to make a case for or against the existence of defensive radicalism as far as these progressive countries are concerned.

As for the rest of Africa, the case is relatively easy. The discrepancies between ideology and practice are wide and obvious. For instance, in the case studies of indigenization policies we saw how indigenization, a potentially progressive phenomenon, is used to facilitate private appropriation, class formation and the dictatorship of the petty bourgeoisie.

Defensive radicalism is not simply something which occurs because some African leaders happen to have decided on defending the status quo by means of ideological mystification. It is an objective necessity of the African situation. African leaders have to make a show of being on the side of the masses. As has been pointed out before, they came to power in the wake of a recent popular movement and their legitimacy as rulers depends on their championship of the cause of the African masses. As the contradictions in the global system develop and the global struggle intensifies, it becomes ever more unlikely for a leadership which is not populist, or which does not at least affect populism, to survive in Africa. The ruling classes of Africa cannot rely exclusively on force to maintain their rule, and the only alternative to force is defensive radicalism. Defensive radicalism is the only way of connecting with the aspirations of the masses, of joining their side so to speak, of plausibly acting as their champions. The realities, of course, limit how one can join the masses, how rulers may mystify. To join the struggle on the side of the African masses, one must necessarily be progressive. To pretend to identify with the struggle of the African masses, one necessarily pretends to hold progressive ideas. The objective situation of the masses is such that the ideas which express their interests, and dominate and orient their struggle, are ideas such as equality and emancipation from exploitation. Quite clearly, defensive radicalism is a necessary feature for the African bourgeoisie — at any rate in those countries in Africa with developing class contradiction.

Just as defensive radicalism arises from the objective situation, so too do differences in the extent of defensive radicalism. For instance, defensive radicalism is more evident in those countries which have less economic growth. A comparison between Kenya and Tanzania throws light on how differences in the degree of defensive radicalism might be explained. Soon after independence, Tanzania started to become more leftist than Kenya. Tanzania's leftward move was dictated by economic necessity, particularly the difficulties she experienced in the early years after independence. To begin with, Tanzania could not find the money to implement her development plan. She had expected that foreign sources would contribute Sh. 1,590 million of her development budget. Unfortunately only a meagre Sh.236 million had been obtained during the first half of the plan period. To absorb the significance of this, one must realize that the projected foreign contribution of Sh.1,590 million was

78% of all development expenditure. Meanwhile the prices of Tanzania's two major export commodities, sisal and cotton, declined by about 35%. A serious drought occurred in 1965 and adversely affected the production of maize, rice and groundnuts, pulses and seed beans. While total employment fell, the cost of living increased. It was in the face of this economic crisis that *The Arusha Declaration* proclaimed the policy of socialism and self-reliance, making a virtue of necessity.

By comparison, Kenya was doing much better. The first plan period (1964-65) went well. The target rate of increase in production was achieved, the planned increase of per capita real consumption was achieved, employment opportunities increased considerably, average wages increased by 30% over the plan period, and the average income of the small farmers increased substantially. So the pressure towards defensive radicalism was much smaller.

CONCLUSION

I will conclude by underlining one significance of Africa's tendency towards defensive radicalism.

Defensive radicalism is a progressive force. Paradoxically, while it allows the bourgeoisie to buy time, it develops the consciousness of the people, reveals the contradictions of the social order by creating expectations which cannot be satisfied in the context of the existing order, and thereby intensifies the class struggle. It develops the consciousness of the masses because the rulers' objective interests demand that their defensive radicalism be given maximum exposure. Yet the process of giving it this exposure necessarily entails the propagation of the values and ideology of the class enemies of the regime. Indeed the propagation of the ideology of defensive radicalism undermines the regime's very *raison d'etre*. Defensive radicalism has a dynamic all its own. To purchase legitimacy in this way is to establish a new criterion of regime performance and legitimacy which becomes a constraint on the regime. It becomes a constraint because defensive radicalism is even more self-defeating when it is not plausible, that is to say plausible in relation to regime performance. So, when a regime is obliged to resort to defensive radicalism, it will in all probability become increasingly progressive. It would appear that Africa's movement in a progressive direction depends not on the development of the forces of production and the increase of the surplus, but on the lack of such development.

To sum up, this brief survey of the ideological development of the African bourgeoisie illustrates the relation between consciousness and social existence. Objective conditions have framed a dilemma for the African bourgeoisie. It cannot maintain its class domination without adopting an ideology which will radicalize the masses and promote revolution.

5

THE DYNAMICS OF SOCIAL FORCES: CAPITALISM OR SOCIALISM IN AFRICA ?

I have examined the dynamics of social forces and have shown that it tends both towards the perpetuation of underdevelopment and towards the intensification of revolutionary pressure from below. My analysis of these dynamics has shown how underdevelopment and revolutionary pressures are related. Indeed one might say that in a sense they are aspects of an integral whole, insofar as the revolutionary pressures are inherent in the conditions of underdevelopment as historically determined in Africa. And yet, from another perspective, underdevelopment and revolutionary pressures are in a relationship of contradiction and active opposition; and this contradiction is straining towards resolution, or a new synthesis at any rate. They are in contradiction in the sense that underdevelopment in Africa is tied to the class structure and class contradictions with the result that the revolutionary pressures from below, which strain towards the resolution of class conflict, are *ipso facto* the potential negation of under-development. In this final chapter, I address myself mainly to the question of the resolution of this contradiction between underdevelopment and revolutionary pressures. This is all the more necessary because to examine the possible resolution of this contradiction is in effect to clarify Africa's prospects of either opting for capitalism or of choosing socialism.

CONDITIONS FOR TRANSITION TO SOCIALISM

Class Consciousness in Africa

A convenient place to start is the development of class consciousness. What are the chances that the revolutionary pressures will take the form of increasing class consciousness ? There are some obstacles to the development of class consciousness amongst the African masses. In the first place, the distortions of capitalism which have been shown to hamper economic growth also impede the development of class consciousness. Insofar as capitalism does not develop the forces of production, the process of proletarianization is necessarily arrested, and the development of certain contradictions is impeded. The distortion and transformation of capitalism into state capitalism depersonalizes and conceals exploitation to a considerable degree. For the wage labourer becomes a civil servant and the interest of capital presents itself as the interest of the nation. Second, some aspects of the condition of the peasantry impede the growth of class consciousness; poor communications and the less obvious visibility of inequality are examples. There is also the fact that the bulk of the African peasantry still has some access to land and still 'work for themselves' — all of which gives them a spurious sense of being masters of their own destiny. Their labour is exploited only 'remotely' by the manipulation of commodity prices. Moreover, for a few of them, poverty is somewhat mitigated by the transfer of resources from the towns through the kinship system. Third, there are the factors of nationalism and tribalism which can impede the development of class consciousness. In the short run, the global class struggle reinforces the African bourgeoisie's ability to contain class consciousness by appeals to nationalism. In addition, on the national level, the growth of class consciousness is also limited by the factional struggles within the bourgeoisie which foster tribalist consciousness (although this latter factor will operate less and less as the bourgeoisie becomes more homogeneous).

On the other side of the ledger, there is the high level of political awareness in Africa created by the nationalist movement. Objective conditions compel the African bourgeoisie to maintain and reinforce this political awareness, even when they have to reduce the effective political participation of the masses. For instance, as the economy stagnates, the bourgeoisie tends to substitute rhetoric for bread and faith for progress, in order to contain frustrated expectations. It also tends to dramatize its heroic achievements against imperialism. This cannot be done without escalating political awareness. Second, the political awareness aroused in the masses is a radical one. Since the masses were originally politicized for the purposes of eliminating the colonial regime, the bourgeoisie used a mobilizing ideology which harped on equality, freedom, emancipation from want and from exploitation. The ideologies which are now being used against neo-colonialism and imperialism must also emphasize these values — even though it is no longer in the interest of the African bourgeoisie to draw attention to them. Third, the massive repression and the process of depoliticization is an enormous asset to the growth of class consciousness, even amongst the peasantry. Fourth, there is the harshness of African poverty, which is in sharp contrast to the people's expectations and to their awareness of the affluence of others.

It would seem that the factors conducive to the growth of class consciousness are more significant than those which serve to contain it. Also, the forces which promote class consciousness will tend to get stronger in the long run, while some of those which mitigate it will tend to grow weaker as time goes on. Unfortunately, even if we were absolutely certain that the forces developing class consciousness were clearly dominant and getting stronger, this would not tell us when and how the growth of class consciousness will precipitate revolution in Africa.

Forces of Production and Prospects of Revolution

Some people will not take kindly to this statement. They will argue that our knowledge of the conditions under which socialist revolution occurs is not so deficient, that even though we cannot predict with accuracy when a socialist revolution will occur, we have some good theory, and some reliable knowledge of the circumstances, (at least some of them), under which socialist revolution *cannot* occur. They could proceed to argue that this theory tells us that the conditions for the occurrence of socialist revolutions in Africa do not yet exist. Their case would rest on the very limited development of productive forces and would continue along the following lines: because the forces of production are so underdeveloped, Africa really has no proletariat and it is the proletariat and proletarian consciousness which makes socialist revolution possible. Because of the underdevelopment of the productive forces, including the most decisive productive force, the proletariat, the contradiction between *social* production and *private* appropriation exists only in the most rudimentary form, and hence Africa is very far from the point when it can be said that the social relations of production have become an intolerable fetter on the productive forces.

On its own terms, this argument makes sense. It is a reasonable expectation that as the forces of production develop under capitalism, class conflict and class consciousness will grow deeper. This is so because the development of capitalism invariably leads to the creation of a large industrial reserve army, an endless chain of crises due to the anarchy inherent in capitalist production, the sharpening of the contradiction between the socialization of production and the private character of appropriation, the growth of monopoly, and an increasing discrepancy between the level of social wants and the standard of living of the proletariat.

Logic is not truth, however. While these expectations have a sound basis, they are not apparently realized — although it is still possible that they may be realized in the very long run. I do not mean that the highly developed capitalist systems do not display evidence supporting specific expectations, such as the crises of production, the existence of a large industrial reserve army and increasing socialization of production. They do. What I mean is that these factors do not seem to have created a class consciousness or class struggle of any exceptional intensity in the most advanced capitalist countries such as the United States, the United Kingdom, Canada, West Germany, Japan, Sweden, Italy and France. None of these countries have in the past generation come anywhere near a socialist revolution. On the other hand, the most profound socialist revolutions have occurred in China, Cuba, Vietnam and the Soviet Union, all of them countries in which the development of capitalism was quite rudimentary. This empirical evidence, which has been provided by history itself, has — beginning with Lenin — compelled a theoretical rebuttal of the assumption that socialist revolution always comes in the wake of the advanced development of productive forces.

This is not to say that the development of productive forces is irrelevant to the prospect of socialism. What I really want to suggest is that the relation between socialist revolution and the development of productive forces is obscure. It would appear that there is a kink in the curve, to borrow an expression from economics. Up to a certain threshold, certainly, the development of productive forces is positively associated with the prospects of socialist revolution. But beyond that threshold, which still remains undefined, the development of productive forces becomes negatively associated with the prospects of socialism. Before the social system reaches that point, economic *stagnation* is itself the catalyst of revolution. Although the threshold may be low, the level of development of productive forces in most African countries is still such that the prospect of a socialist revolution does exist. As we saw in our analysis of social forces, the impulses of Africa's radicalization are largely rooted in its economic underdevelopment and all its associated phenomena, such as the meagre material base of its bourgeoisie, depoliticization and so on. Even for those who hold more orthodox views on this matter, the position taken here should not seem particularly far-fetched; I do not believe that it is as fundamentally different from the orthodox view as it seems. For when we analyze the orthodox view, it suggests that revolutionary consciousness arises out of the following essential elements: (a) the existence of poverty, in the physical sense of low living standards and lack of elementary necessities; (b) the existence of poverty in the social sense of workers' living standards lagging behind social wants; and (c) a consciousness of these two facts and active hostility to the social groups and institutions responsible for them. Once we isolate the essentials of revolutionary consciousness in this manner, it is readily apparent that it is not in the least implausible to posit their existence in post-colonial Africa. In the course of my analysis of the dynamics of social forces, I have shown the objective conditions which politicize the physical and social poverty of the African masses. Indeed, I have shown that the African bourgeoisie is trapped in contradictions which compel it to contribute to this politicization.

The Revolutionary Class: Workers or Peasants ?

There is another aspect of the relation between the development of productive forces and socialist revolution which deserves attention. This is the question of the relative revolutionary potential of workers and peasants. The view which makes socialist revolution contingent on the very advanced development of productive forces goes with the belief that only the workers, the proletariat, are truly revolutionary. Those who make this assertion are not necessarily all saying the same thing. Sometimes, this assertion is really a short-hand description of how the development of productive forces generates revolutionary consciousness. More specifically, what is being said is that revolutionary consciousness is something which arises out of the protracted acting out of the contradictions of capitalism, and that the revolutionary class which these processes necessarily create can only be the proletariat. When the assertion is made in this sense, it is not very interesting and remains an abstract claim. If one seeks to go beyond this formal truth, one has to criticise the theoretical and empirical validity of the notion that socialist revolution comes if, and only if, the developments specified in the assertion under review occur. I have already done this in a highly abbreviated way by arguing that socialist revolutions have in fact occurred only in economically backward capitalist countries and never in any of the highly advanced capitalist systems.

The assertion under review usually refers to the comparative suscep-tibility of workers and peasants to radicalization. The particular arguments advanced in favour of the worker being more 'available' for radicalization vary somewhat. Usually they contain one or more of the following points: (a) the development of capitalism necessarily goes hand in hand with the atomization of society, which is alienating for all, but particularly so for workers who must sell themselves to the capitalist; (b) the peasant, especially in Africa, might be said to own some means of production however meagre, but the worker has nothing but his labour power and is totally available for exploitation; (c) the peasant is self-employed and so is more immune to the upheavals of the crises of capitalism; (d) the social setting of the peasant is, to use Durkheim's categories, characterized by mechanical solidarity while that of the worker is characterized by organic solidarity, and this makes the worker more susceptible to alienation and radicalization; (e) the worker is in a social setting in which inequality is more visible — for instance he is more likely to notice income and wage differentials, and the differences in the living conditions of the workers and the bourgeoisie.

There is much to be said for these points. In fact, I accept them as essentially correct. Nevertheless, they do not warrant the conclusion that only workers can be revolutionary. The conclusion that they warrant is merely that the worker is more likely to attain revolutionary consciousness than the peasant. Even then, the empirical validity of this conclusion is open to question. As has been pointed out before, socialist revolutions have tended to occur in those countries where the forces of production are less developed and a good number of these revolutions have had a specifically peasant base — for example China, Cambodia, Vietnam, and Guinea-Bissau. In short, there is no case for denying the revolutionary potential of the peasantry — including the African peasantry. I will leave the issue at that and return to the original problem of how the contradiction between underdevelopment and revolutionary pressures is likely to be resolved.

THE PROSPECTS FOR SOCIALISM IN AFRICA

Africa's Progressive Countries

Will the revolutionary pressures mounting in Africa culminate in socialist revolutions ? I will begin by considering the handful of progressive countries, namely Angola, Mozambique and Guinea-Bissau. If one argues that these countries are already socialist countries, then of course the question does not arise. However, such an assumption is highly problematical. The leadership of these countries is clearly a petty bourgeoisie, and there are clearly some contradictions between this petty bourgeois class and the masses. As far as I can see, some of these leaders themselves recognize this contradiction and do not present themselves as socialist regimes; instead they make the more limited claim that they are committed to socialism and well on the way to building a socialist society. Meanwhile, this revolutionary petty bourgeoisie is now confronting its moment of truth. As Cabral aptly puts it in *Revolution in Guinea*, this revolutionary petty bourgeoisie must decide whether

'to give free rein to its natural tendencies to become more bourgeois, to permit the development of a bureaucratic and intermediary bourgeoisie in the commercial cycle, in order to transform itself into a national pseudo-bourgeoisie, that is to say in order to negate the revolution and necessarily ally itself with imperialist capital.'

This is what seems to have happened in Algeria, where the promise of a progressive revolution has not been realized.

The alternative is for the revolutionary petty bourgeoisie to be capable of 'committing suicide as a class in order to be reborn as revolutionary workers, completely identified with the deepest aspirations of the people to which they belong'. Angola, Guinea-Bissau and Mozambique appear to be following this path.

Perhaps the phrase 'committing suicide' is unfortunate. The petty bourgeoisie does not really commit suicide. What it does is to recognize that its true interest lies in promoting the revolution instead of becoming an agent of imperialism. It recognizes and seizes the opportunity for a great historical role instead of remaining historically irrelevant. Above all, it recognizes that, being divorced from production, its political power can never really be consolidated, for, in the post-colonial societies of Africa, the material base of political power belongs either to the metropolitan bourgeoisies of the imperialist countries or to the local workers and peasants who are the classes actually involved in production. In identifying with the people, the revolutionary petty bourgeoisie also preserves the power which it won through the nationalist struggle. It should be added that it is not really a matter of chance whether the revolutionary petty bourgeoisie recognizes these opportunities or not. In all three instances where they appear to have recognized it (i.e. Angola, Mozambique and Guinea-Bissau), the nationalist liberation struggle was protracted, bitter and violent, and its ideology was socialist or at any rate heavily impregnated with elements of socialism. Waging armed struggle with an essentially socialist ideology, over a long period, gave the leadership an exceptional ideological clarity — and this is why they are able to recognize the necessity of taking the side of the masses. In Algeria there was also a violent and protracted armed struggle, but its ideology was much less socialist and the struggle does not seem to have conferred on its leaders much ideological clarity or even coherence. As for the ongoing struggle in Zimbabwe, it displays much the same ideological fuzziness as the Algerian one. If Zimbabwe were to become independent in the immediate future, the chances are that the revolution would be betrayed.

Even for those countries whose leaders are promoting socialism, the future is still full of perils. One danger is the presence of reactionary elements within the revolutionary leadership itself. There are factions within these leaderships who would have preferred the leadership to become bourgeois and to get on with enjoying the fruits of the nationalist struggle. Such factions will masquerade as socialist, bide their time and try to seize power when they sense an opportunity. Such attempts have already been made in Mozambique and Angola. It is to be expected that there will be more attempts of this nature as the revolutions press on with the elimination of the remaining vestiges of class contradiction.

The second kind of danger is more subtle, but no less serious. The danger is that the pressure of circumstances may undermine their sense of purpose and lead them into unnecessary, counter-productive brutality. What are these circumstances? First, imperialism will do everything to subvert these regimes. Second, they will be under pressure from the reactionary African countries which surround them. Third, they will have to deal with the reactionaries within their own leaderships. In addition to all this, there will be the problems of mobilizing and radicalizing the peasants, of disengaging from the exploitative relationships with imperialism that were created in the colonial period, and of liberating the productive forces. It is just possible that the revolutionary leaderships may find themselves preoccupied with bare survival and unable to do much about advancing productivity or constructing socialism. They may be overwhelmed by frustration and a sense of impotence and may seek release in some forms of symbolic success. It is all too easy to seek scapegoats; and then, enemies of the regime are found everywhere, the rhetoric gets more violent, and the firing squads march in the morning.

Africa's Less Progressive Countries

In predicting what is likely to happen in these countries, we cannot rely on an analysis of the development of class consciousness. As I have already pointed out, no one really knows, as yet, when and how the growth of class consciousness precipitates revolution. Fortunately, it is unnecessary for us to speculate along these lines because there is a characteristic of the African situation which gives us more tangible insights into the prospects of socialist revolution in the countries under consideration. The characteristic in question is Africa's immense statism and the primacy of politics which is associated with it.

The aspect of this statism which is most pregnant with significance is the focus of so many people's energies on the struggle for state power. What this really means is that a revolutionary situation exists — although it does not mean that the revolution is taking place. A revolutionary situation exists throughout Africa because the objective conditions are such that the class struggle presents itself immediately as the struggle for state power. It is desirable to avoid confusing questions of quality with questions of quantity. When I say that a revolutionary situation exists in Africa, I am talking about the character of the class struggle, (its quality), not about its intensity, (its quantity). Its intensity may well be quite limited. However that is beside the point; a revolutionary situation exists nevertheless, inasmuch as the class struggle focuses on state power.

To be sure, much of the struggle for state power in Africa is limited to the factions of the African bourgeoisie and this intra-class struggle for control of state power is not revolutionary. However while not itself revolutionary, it stands an excellent chance of spilling out beyond present class lines, and galvanizing the weak revolutionary class struggle which already exists into an intense revolutionary struggle. This will happen if a faction of the bourgeoisie under pressure decides to mobilize the exploited class *as a class.* In the factional struggle for hegemony, factions of the bourgeoisie usually try to mobilize and involve the exploited in their causes. Generally they do not involve them as a class, but rather by appeals to common identities such as tribe, religious group or geographical area, which cut across class lines. But if the exploited are involved as a class, the struggle will become a revolutionary struggle proper.

Why should such a situation materialize ? How would it materialize ? It certainly would not be the product of random events; on the contrary, it would occur according to objective conditions. What are these conditions ? The major factor is the colonial legacy of statism and all those forces which are reinforcing it, particularly the pursuit of development in the absence of substantial private capital and the drive of the African bourgeoisie to consolidate its material base by translating its political power into economic power. To some extent, statism is a negation of capitalism, and its concomitant ideology necessarily has a high socialist content. The factor which has made the ideology of the statist economies in Africa particularly 'socialist' is the extension of statism for the specific purpose of consolidating the material base of the new bourgeoisie. As has been shown, this goes hand in hand with the tendency to nationalize more and more. Even though nationalizations and such related measures for extending public control may conceal capitalist motives, they have to be justified with essentially socialist values. In this sense, it might be said that objective conditions are moving Africa to the left. As we have already seen, there is hardly any African country which does not profess some form of socialism. That the African bourgeoisies use the language of socialism to conceal capitalist values is true but irrelevant. What matters is that they are obliged to choose this particular form of dissimulation — to adopt ideas which are ultimately incompatible with the survival of their class. If all this is correct, we must conclude that even the hegemonic faction of a bourgeoisie in any particular country is already facilitating the conversion of the struggle for state power into a revolution. So it is highly probable that a particularly embattled and dissatisfied faction of a ruling bourgeoisie or petty bourgeoisie, as the case may be, could carry this further, stand on a more rigorously socialist ideology and try to mobilize the masses to fight as a class.

Such a state of affairs could occur as a result of purely opportunistic manoeuvres by a faction of the ruling class which had decided to fight under the banner of socialism. This faction might promote revolutionary struggles as a strategic move in its quest for power, hoping that as soon as the revolution takes hold, it would quickly be de-radicalized. In all probability such fraudulent socialist revolutions will occur. But it makes no difference whether they fail or succeed. For if fraudulent revolutions fail, it is back to the status quo, with perhaps a little more repression. If they succeed, it is still back to the status quo with a few new faces at the top and even more repression to deal with frustrated expectations. There is just a chance that, once launched, such a fraudulent socialist revolution may elude the control of both the old regime and the 'revolutionaries' who launched it, develop a dynamic of its own and move toward a genuine socialist revolution. However, this is not a likely event.

The second possibility is that a socialist revolution may occur as a result of a genuine conversion of a faction of the ruling bourgeoisie or petty bourgeoisie to socialism. Now it is true that socialism is antithetical to the objective interests of the bourgeoisie as a class. Nevertheless, factions of a bourgeoisie may be so alienated as to turn against their own class; factions of the bourgeoisie may be radicalized to the point of accepting socialism. In Africa, there is an especially good chance that some elements of the petty bourgeoisie may be so radicalized. Let us consider how this could happen. To begin with, we have to bear in mind that the contradictions of capitalism in the Third World, especially in Africa, are uniquely poignant: for instance, cities of wretchedly poor countries are immobilized by traffic jams; the insecurity of life and property as a result of 'crimes' which are really expressions of the class struggle; the bourgeoisie having to endure enormous inconveniences and frustrations because regulations cannot be enforced due to the widespread corruption which arises from the insane quest for wealth. Such contradictions could bring home even to elements within the ruling class the realization that the system has to go. Such a realization could easily come to those marginal elements within the bourgeoisie who, unable to compete effectively, have become alienated. The interaction of alienation and grotesque contradictions could easily deepen their radicalism and give them ideological clarity so that people in this position could eventually become socialists. This is how the leaders of the socialist revolution in the less progressive countries of Africa are likely to emerge.

Character of The Probable Revolution

I will now turn to a brief consideration of the character of these probable socialist revolutions. From what I have said about the circumstances under which these revolutions are likely to occur, it should be clear that, paradoxical as it may seem, their occurrence will depend not so much on the state of development of class contradictions as on the dynamics of intra-class competition within the bourgeoisie. To avoid misunderstanding, I should emphasize that I am not saying that class contradictions do not 'determine' the occurrence of revolution. They do. For it is class contradictions which create the conditions under which (a) even the hegemonic faction of the bourgeoisie is obliged to promote the radicalization of popular consciousness; (b) fractions of the bourgeoisie become profoundly alienated and radicalized; and (c) intra-class competition within the ruling class creates what I have called a revolutionary situation. When I say that the occurrence of the revolution depends on the dynamics of intra-class competition, I am merely saying that the immediate trigger of the revolution is likely to be the radicalization of petty bourgeois elements and that the revolution will at first appear in disguise as an intra-class struggle before it truly reveals itself.

Because of this, the revolution is unlikely to entail protracted preparatory mobilization and politicization of the masses. And it is unlikely that the seizure of power will be achieved by the physical force or economic power of the masses. This is all the more so because the legacy of statism makes the seizure of state power the established method of resolving serious political differences within the ruling class. The seizure of state power is likely to be carried out in the way it has always been since independence. i.e. It will be done, not by involving the masses, but by confining the struggle largely to the ruling class. The tendency to do this is increased by the fact that the revolutionaries would be reacting most immediately to intra-class contradictions.

If this is true, then we can make two further predictions about the character of these probable revolutions. First, there is a good chance that the revolutions will become reactionary, to the point of virtually recreating the old order shortly after they occur. Having come to power, the marginality and alienation of the leaders of the revolution will disappear and their consciousness will tend to change accordingly. They may well revert to their petty bourgeois mentality and de-radicalize the revolution.

The second prediction is this: even assuming the best intentions on the part of the 'revolutionaries', the revolution is not likely to go very deep, in the sense of completely overturning existing relations of production and universalizing the proletarian condition. This is so because, although the revolution will be made in the name of the masses (as we have seen), it is not likely that the masses will play a more than marginal role. In so far as the masses are involved, it will be only the urban element, the workers. In the final analysis a revolution is as radical as its social base — one should not confuse the social background of the leaders of the revolution with the social base of the revolution itself. Even if the urban proletariat were thoroughly mobilized and involved, the depth and radicalism of the revolution would still be questionable. Unlike workers in the bourgeois countries, the workers in Africa represent a relatively privileged group in comparison to the peasantry. For instance, the ratio of urban to rural incomes in Africa is usually above 5 : 1. In addition to this income advantage, the urban population enjoys a virtual monopoly of social amenities such as water supply, electricity, schools, good roads etc. The consequent contradiction between the rural and urban areas manifests itself to some extent as a contradiction between workers and peasants. To all appearances this contradiction is not really antagonistic, but it could easily begin to develop in that direction. Be that as it may, the point is that an African revolution with a proletarian social base would represent a less fundamental change than one with a peasant base. It would reflect the contradictions between town and country, peasant and worker, and would have tendencies which are not conducive to the full emancipation of the peasantry.

There is another reason why it would be most desirable to have a peasant-based revolution. If socialist revolution is to put an end to under-development, it must accomplish the task of at once abolishing capitalism and socializing production and also breaking exploitative ties with imperialism. The breaking of exploitative ties with imperialism will be a particularly difficult task. The key obstacle in this respect may well be the consumption pattern of the urban African — bourgeois and worker alike — and not, as one might have expected, the resistance of imperialism to the severing of these ties. For if the exploitative ties with imperialism are seriously attacked, this will seriously affect or even end altogether the supply of those goods and services which give a spurious air of commodious living in urban Africa and which imperialism uses to

105

hold Africa in bondage. The peasantry is the only social group which is almost totally free from this bondage. It cannot make much difference to the African peasant if his country's supply of aeroplanes, tarred roads, refrigerators, gabardine trousers, Uncle Ben's rice, tinned milk, sardines, jeans and tooth-paste is interrupted or even stopped, for African peasants are rarely in a position to consume such goods. How men make a revolution is determined in some measure by what they are. And it is too easy to assume that people addicted to the goods and services obtainable through ties with imperialism will not be reluctant about dismantling some of these ties. The spirit may be willing, but the flesh may well be weak. Unfortunately, there is very little chance that peasant-based socialist revolutions will occur in Africa. The chances of worker-based socialist revolutions are somewhat better. But, as I have argued, the best chance of all is for socialist revolutions engineered by a faction of the ruling class and involving workers only to a very limited extent. These will necessarily be moderate socialist revolutions.

AFRICA'S REAL CHOICE: SOCIALISM OR BARBARISM

What if socialist revolutions do not occur? If the contradiction between underdevelopment and the revolutionary pressures which we have identified is not resolved in a socialist revolution, what alternative paths of development are there?

One possibility for the resolution of the contradiction will be accelerated capitalist economic growth and the consequent weakening of the revolutionary pressures. We might place this in an opposition to the first option (socialist revolution) and say that, in this case, what happens is the resolution of the contradiction between underdevelopment and revolutionary pressures in favour of underdevelopment by a capitalist revolution, so to speak. Is there an inconsistency here? Why does one talk of the contradiction being resolved in favour of *underdevelopment* when what would actually happen in this case is a 'capitalist revolution', meaning accelerated capitalist economic growth? As will be clear shortly, there is no inconsistency in this. In a few countries such as Nigeria, Kenya, Algeria and Egypt, it is just possible that, despite all the forces I have outlined in this book which are operating to hinder capitalist economic growth, there will be sufficient economic growth to ease the revolutionary pressures and even to develop a national bourgeoisie which can actually both control the economy and keep its hold on state power. Nevertheless being capitalist and constrained by all the factors we have enumerated, this economic growth could only increase the surplus without moving the system away from underdevelopment. And of course there is no chance at all that it will increase the surplus to anything remotely near the point when the African country involved could be said to be 'catching up' with the bourgeois countries. The possibility under consideration ('capitalist revolution') would still perpetuate underdevelopment by inhibiting the factors which alone can overcome it.

The third historic possibility which lies before Africa is a march to fascism. This could come about in a situation where there was protracted economic stagnation, but not yet revolution. During such a period, the contradictions of underdevelopment would be acted out and indeed made all the more dramatic precisely because of the long drawn-out economic stagnation. But how would the contradictions be dealt with, how would the desperation of the wretched masses be contained? By bread and circuses? Circuses perhaps, but not bread because this would simply not be available. But one thing that would surely be needed in ever increasing quantities in this situation would be repression. As the economic stagnation persisted, the masses would become more wretched and desperate and the contradictions would develop. Wretchedness and desperation would lead peasants to subversion, workers to industrial action, and the lumpen-proletariat to robbery and violence. Punitive expeditions would then be sent out to liquidate whole villages, armed robbers would be punished by public executions, and other crimes against property would be dealt with by imposing sanctions of exceptional harshness. Striking workers would be chased by police dogs, locked out, starved out, shot at. Any person or group of persons who looked like being a rallying point against the system would be summarily liquidated. All this is already happening. And things are likely to get worse, if only because repression demoralizes the country, impedes productivity and ties up too much of the meagre surplus in servicing coercive institutions. So we have a vicious circle promising ever more blood and sweat. It would appear that the choice for Africa is not between capitalism and socialism after all, but between socialism and barbarism. Which will it be ?

REFERENCES

Chapter I

1.   Karl Marx and Frederick Engels, *Manifesto of The Communist Party*, in Marx and Engels, *Selected Works*, Progress Publishers (Moscow, 1969), Vol.1, p.112.
2.   Karl Marx, *Grundrisse*, Penguin, (London, 1973), p.156.
3.   Karl Marx, *Capital: A Critical Analysis of Capitalist Production.* Progress Publishers, (Moscow, 1954), Vol.1, pp.174.
4.   *Ibid.*
5.   *Ibid*, p.175-6.
6.   Karl Marx, *Critique of the Gotha Programme*, in Marx and Engels, op. cit.,

Vol. 3, p.13.

7. Karl Marx, *A Contribution to the Critique of Political Economy*, Progress Publishers, (Moscow, 1970), p.20.

8. For those countries classified as the least developed of the African countries only a 2.5% fall in prices is needed to qualify for compensation.

9. For a short but useful commentary on STABEX see Alan Rake, 'STABEX; How Effective Will It Really Be?', *African Development*, Vol.9, No. 6. June 1975, pp.23-25. For a longer and excellent commentary see Johan Galtung, 'The Lome Convention and Neo-Capitalism', scheduled for publication in *African Review*.

10. For evidence of increasing monopolization of the control of technology see *US Government Science Indicators 1972: Report of the National Science Board*, US Government Printer, (Washington, January 1973); OECD, *Gaps in Technology: Analytic Report*, OECD, (Paris, 1970).

Chapter II

1. It is important to bear in mind the special usage of this term here.

2. ILO, *Employment, Incomes and Equality: A Strategy for Increasing Productive Employment in Kenya*, ILO Office, (Geneva, 1972), p.74-5.

3. Government of Kenya, *Statistical Abstracts 1975*, Government Printer, (Nairobi, 1975).

4. GATT, *International Trade 1973/74* (Geneva, 1974); UN, *Yearbook of International Trade Statistics 1972/73*, (New York, 1974). For the purposes of these calculations, Africa excludes South Africa; the industrialized capitalist countries' share is for Western Europe, EEC, EFTA, US and Canada; communist block consists of Albania, Bulgaria, Czechoslovakia, German Democratic Republic, Hungary, Poland, Rumania, USSR, China, Mongolia, North Korea and North Vietnam.

5. H.M.A. Onitiri, 'The International Aspects of Economic Independence', in D. P. Ghai (Ed.), *Economic Independence in Africa*, East African Literature Bureau, (Nairobi, 1973), p.37-8.

6. For information on the settlement schemes see Government of Kenya, *Economic Survey, 1971*, Government Printer, (Nairobi, 1971); *Development Plan 1970-74*, Government Printer, (Nairobi, 1969), pp.201-211.

7. *Development Plan 1970-74*, p.199.

8. *Ibid.*, p.192.

9. *Ibid.*, p.193.

10. Colin Leys, *Underdevelopment in Kenya: The Political Economy of Neo-Colonialism 1964-71*, University of California Press, (Berkeley and Los Angeles, 1974), p.93.

11. ILO, *Employment, Incomes and Inequality*, p.35-7.

12. *Ibid.*, p.37.

13. *Development Plan 1970-74*, p.316.

14. Colin Leys, *op. cit.*, p.165.
15. ILO, *op. cit.*, p.442.
16. *Ibid.*, p.100-1.
17. Leys, *op. cit.*, p.165.
18. Federal Military Government of Nigeria, *Supplement to Official Gazette Extraordinary*, Vol. 58, Feb. 28, 1972.
19. e.g., General Gowon as quoted in *New Nigerian*, October 3, 1972; State Governor Usman Farouk, *New Nigerian*, June 13, 1973.
20. *The Daily Times*, June 18, 1974.
21. Ministry of Economic Affairs and Development Planning, *Analysis of Accounts of Parastatals 1966-1973*, (Dar es Salaam, 1974), p.1.
22. Quoted by G.M. Chamungwana in 'The Parastatal System in Tanzania', *Rasilimali: Tanzania Investment Outlook*, Tanzania Investment Bank, (Dar es Salaam).
23. United Republic of Tanzania, *The Annual Plan for 1970/71*, Government Printer, (Dar es Salaam, 1970).
24. Minister of Finance, Budget Speech, June 12, 1974; June 13, 1975.

ZED PRESS is a new socialist publisher of books on the Third
World. Our first series are: Imperialism and Revolution, Women
in the Third World, Africa, the Middle East and Asia.

Our books are both introductory texts and more advanced
analyses of the complex forms of oppression which Third World
revolutionary forces are struggling to overcome. Most of our
authors use Marxism as their basis for coming to grips with
political history, with the way the world is structured and with
what the future holds. Our writers are people, many of whom
are in active opposition to the forces of imperialist oppression
in its local and international manifestations. We intend our
authors to be equally from the Third World and from the West.

ZED PRESS is committed to taking radical literature out of the
studies of the academics and into the hands of a much wider
circle of intellectuals who feel the need to understand our contradiction and crisis-ridden world. We will encourage manuscripts
which do this.

We aim to distribute ZED's books as widely as possible, especially
in the Third World. We want to get our books directly to those
involved in anti-imperialist struggles. We have a network of
representatives, and are building up a direct mail order service
to make our books accessible anywhere in the world. We are
therefore willing to help other radical publishers in providing a
more comprehensive distribution of their titles in the Third
World, in addition to originating our own titles.

ZED PRESS is financially independent and not tied to any
political faction. Our aim is to encourage broad debate in a
Marxist and socialist framework, to promote radical knowledge
and to build up a climate of opinion favourable to liberation
everywhere.

OTHER BOOKS AVAILABLE FROM ZED PRESS

(Please note: UK prices quoted in sterling; prices for rest of the world in US dollars.)

Annerstedt (Jan) & Gustavsson (Rolf) **Towards a New International Division of Labour?** Pb £1.95/$3.75 (Not available in Sandinavia)

Caldwell (Malcolm) **The Wealth of Some Nations** Hb £5.00/$10.00

Davis (Uri) **Israel: Utopia Incorporated** Hb £5.00/$10.00

Eisen Bergman (Arlene) **Women in Vietnam** Pb £2.75/$5.40 (Not available in North America)

Elliott (David) **Thailand: Origins of Military Rule** Hb £5.95/$12.95

Hirson (Baruch) **Soweto: Roots of a Revolution?** Hb (In preparation)

Kiernan (Victor) **America — The Imperial Record** Hb £6.95/$12.95

Mandel (Ernest) **From Class Society to Communism** Hb $10.50; Pb $3.95 (Available Third World only)

Nabudere (Wadada) **The Political Economy of Imperialism** Hb £7.75/$15.50 (Pb distributed by Tanzania Publishing House in Africa)

Peoples Press **With Freedom in their Eyes (Angola)** Pb £2.50/$5.00 (Not available in North America)

Peoples Press **Our Roots Are Still Alive** Pb £2.95 (Not available in North America)

Probert (Belinda) **The Northern Ireland Crisis** Hb £6.50/$12.50

Rodinson (Maxime) **Marxism and the Muslim World** Hb £8.75/$18.50

Samir Amin **The Arab Nation: Nationalism and Class Struggles** Hb £6.50/$12.75

Seidman (Ann and Neva) **U.S. Multinationals in Southern Africa** Pb £4.95 (Not available in Africa and North America)